'Nora Lever has produced a fascinating account of life as a diplomat's wife in Saudi Arabia before, during, and after the Gulf War. Highly accomplished in her own right, she put her career on hold to support her husband, Allan's, ambassadorial assignment to a country where women are blocked from even the simplest of activities. Yet she found a way to contribute, in her own way, teaching English as a foreign language to young women.

One might well assume that a posting to a country blessed with enormous oil revenues would be one to envy. That would be wrong. Saudi Arabia is a hostile environment for women. Driving, even shopping without male accompaniment, is forbidden, forcing on wives of diplomats a cloistered social life, generally among their peers.

The Levers made a great team, as those of us who travelled to the kingdom on business can attest. That *the prime minister* asked them to extend their time there is indicative of how valuable their service was to Canada.'

— HUGH MULLINGTON, *former president,*
Canadian Commercial Corporation

DIPLOMACY
AND
FRIENDSHIP

Ambassador's Wife *in* Gulf War Riyadh

A Memoir

NORA HAZLEWOOD LEVER

Words Indeed Publishing
Toronto

Words Indeed Publishing, Toronto

www.wordsindeed.ca | info@wordsindeed.ca

ISBN: 978-0-9865166-8-9

The publisher has made every effort to contact sources
for this volume. We apologize for any errors or omissions.
Please let us know of any relevant information.

Library and Archives Canada Cataloguing in Publication

Lever, Nora Hazlewood, author
Diplomacy and friendship : ambassador's wife in Gulf War Riyadh/
Nora Hazlewood Lever
ISBN 978-0-9865166-8-9 (softcover)
1. Lever, Nora Hazlewood—Diaries. 2. Ambassadors' spouses—
Canada—Diaries. 3. Persian Gulf War, 1991. 4. Riyadh
(Saudi Arabia)—History—20th century. I. Title.

FC631.L48A3 2017   327.710092   C2017-901878-7

Cover + book design, photo research + editing:

Anne Vellone, www.vellonedesign.com

Copyediting & publishing: John Parry, www.wordsindeed.ca

Printing: Andora Graphics, www.andoragraphics.com

Text printed on 30% PCW recycled content and FSC certified stock
First edition printed and bound in Canada 2017

For Allan, whose appointment as
Canadian ambassador to the Kingdom of Saudi Arabia
made possible my story of our years in Riyadh,
and for our children — John, David, Gillian,
and Christopher — who lovingly kept in touch with us,
through war and peace, with their faxes,
letters, telephone calls, and visits

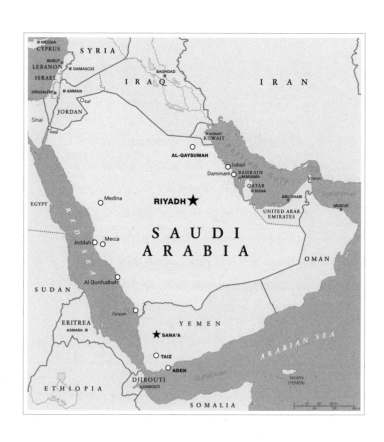

Diplomacy (from the Greek διπλωμα, *"official document conferring a privilege"*) is the art and practice of conducting negotiations between representatives of states. It usually refers to international diplomacy, the conduct of international relations through the intercession of professional diplomats with regard to issues of peace-making, trade, war, economics, culture, environment, and human rights.

— *Wikipedia,* The Free Encyclopedia

In the Foreign Service we often encounter different and to some perhaps distressing local customs, practices and laws. We can accept some of these local practices in the context of cultural sovereignty. Others are perceived as abuses of human rights. How does the abaya and what it represents fit into the picture? **Nora Lever** voices her own dilemma about women in Saudi society sincerely and candidly.

— *Liaison 6* (April 1990), no. 6, 17

Traditional Saudi wooden door

CONTENTS

FOREWORD
A Note about Nora

Stevie Cameron, CM DD

Nora Lever's absorbing account of her years in the Middle East as the wife of Canada's ambassador to Saudi Arabia reminds me of the women travellers of the 1800s who ignored convention and fell in love with places considered dangerous and completely inappropriate for a woman. Gertrude Bell, the most famous of these intrepid explorers, wrote a brilliant book about her years in the Middle East. (I remember my grandmother reading it — more than once — with tears rolling down her face.) And there was Mary Kingsley who travelled in West Africa and wrote about her adventures as well. Nora's experiences, even in this modern age, fit easily into this genre.

When her husband, Allan, a senior official at External Affairs, was offered the opportunity to serve as Canada's ambassador to Saudi Arabia, Nora went with him, even though she had an extraordinary job as Principal Clerk of the Table for the House of Commons, a position she will explain in the pages that follow. As a political reporter back in those days, I would see Nora, dressed in a black robe with a stiff white collar, ready to advise Bev Koester, the Clerk of the House. Of course, I never had the nerve to speak to her.

Nora's diaries, carefully kept over many years, form the substance of this book. She describes the arcane duties of a spouse in a country where women gather together on social occasions while the men stand apart, mixing only with each other. It may sound odd to us now, but the diaries offer lively accounts of merry gatherings with the other wives of diplomats.

Given her valuable experience in Canadian politics and government, Nora successfully manages the two sides of Saudi hospitality — the formal government events as well as the parties put together by the women to celebrate friendship, weddings, new babies, birthdays, and holidays. The whole issue of clothing is a major concern for newcomers from a Western country; in her case, Nora bought an abaya, a long, black cloak-like dress that covers the body and a black scarf that covers the hair.

Few books bring us into such an intimate and surprising view of Saudi Arabia; this very readable book helps us to understand its people and to understand how foreigners feel about the country. The fine collection of photographs — including a picture of Nora in the abaya — make the book even more interesting and more personal. She has changed my view of Saudi Arabia. Not completely, mind you — but she helps the reader to understand it and her affection for the country.

Saudi Arabian desert camels

Picnic in the desert, *1992*

PREFACE
From Diary to Book

ONE CHILLY SPRING EVENING in May 1998 my husband, Allan, and I had dinner with an old friend whom we hadn't seen since her husband died a few years earlier. Until recently, Dorothy had been an active artist, specializing in fine silver jewellery, but sadly her macular degeneration had made such fine craftsmanship impossible. Not to worry, though. This strong woman, now in her eighties, was painting with watercolours and oils, inviting friends for dinners, and proudly experimenting with new recipes.

During our conversation, Dorothy expressed great interest in the time that Allan and I had spent in Saudi Arabia. "Have you considered writing a book?" she asked me.

I responded guiltily: even though I had kept a diary of our fascinating experiences there around the time of the Gulf War, the task of organizing the material and trying to present it in an appealing way overwhelmed me.

Dorothy's observation made me think. "You know," she murmured, "when we confess our sins, we should be conscious of sins of *omission* as much as sins of *commission*."

Well, here goes. I will try to pull together a few of the interesting moments we had in the mysterious and fascinating country known as the Kingdom of Saudi Arabia. We loved our time there, despite the stresses of the Gulf War, which also added spice to our already exotic time there. Our many Saudi friends, as well as others in the diplomatic corps there, are precious to us, and it is truly a pleasure to reflect again on such a remarkable experience.

While in Riyadh I sent letters to Allan's parents and to each of our children, using mail service when readily available and sending faxes too. This was before the amazing era of e-mail, Facebook, Face-time, Instagram, texts, etc.! But I did use a computer to write in my diary from time to time as well — mostly when Allan was busy with visiting Canadian businessmen coupled with Saudi government officials while women were excluded.

There were rich experiences to record as we became acquainted with the Saudi culture, the hospitality of Arab traditions, and the dry desert environment where we lived.

The days of increasing tension during the buildup to the Gulf War led me to write about the details that were taking over our lives, so the diary moves almost at a daily pace as war approached.

But there were also times when I had the time to reflect on the books I was reading and on what I could possibly do professionally if time and fortune allowed.

A FEW YEARS HAVE GONE BY. I have just read our neighbour Tony van Straubenzee's lively memoir, *Rind in the Marmalade: A Headhunter's Tales,* which inspires me to back up a bit to tell you what I was doing in the years leading up to our Saudi adventure. I'll just dip into my diary. Let's see ...

INTRODUCTION
Officer of Parliament

IN 1975, WE WERE LIVING IN OTTAWA with all four of our children in school and my mother, a retired high-school English teacher, available to help. I was studying for a master's degree in political science at Carleton University and had worked for two years with Professors John Sigler, Janice Stein, Blema Steinberg, and Albert Legault on a Canada Council research project in international relations. The House of Commons held a Canada-wide competition to find several bilingual Clerks to administer and offer advice to its standing committees, and I obtained one of the posts. Now I was able to work in the Committees Branch and complete my master's degree as well.

Over the next 14 years, the House of Commons gave me superb training in planning, procedures, the French language, and the complex nuances of human interaction — to say nothing of facial recognition and the handling of delicate egos! All of this would stand me in good stead when External Affairs sent my husband and me to Saudi Arabia in 1989.

Planning *and* Procedures

THE CLERK ADMINISTERS THE COMMITTEE: arranges for witnesses to appear; prepares the agenda, writes minutes, and oversees production and translation of the resulting texts; and co-ordinates the activities of the research staff. The Clerk also offers procedural advice to the Chair and members, so I could enjoy the fun and games of procedural points of order and various motions and amendments thereto.

I started at Fisheries and Environment, which was examining industrial mercury poisoning in the (First Nations) Grassy Narrows Reserve, near Kenora, Ontario — still a devastating concern today. Committee member Joe Clark was a new PC MP for High River, Alberta, and his hands trembled whenever the Chair asked him to speak, but he was a fast learner — prime minister in 1979.

Later I was Clerk for External Affairs, under Chair Herb Breau, Liberal MP from New Brunswick (Pierre Trudeau was in power). North–South Relations, or international development, was a hot topic, and we travelled to the Philippines, Hong Kong, South Korea (a newly developing country), Bangladesh, and Singapore. Ivan Head, director of the International Development Research Centre (IRDC), helped me plan this complex operation.

One time I needed to schedule Secretary of State for External Affairs Don Jamieson to appear to make a statement and answer questions. My husband was his executive assistant; when I called the minister's office, Allan said, "We'll see."

"Indeed we will," I replied, "and we look forward to your arrival at exactly 10 a.m. on February 10th." Needless to say, Mr Jamieson appeared on time, with Allan sitting directly behind him (and opposite my seat beside the Chair).

My final assignment as a Clerk was to the Special Committee on Fiscal Arrangements, under Herb Breau, and I had to make travel plans and schedule witnesses across the country.

But before we completed this study, a new Clerk of the House of Commons, Dr Beverley Koester, took office in 1979 and invited me to become his executive assistant for a year. Through summer 1979, Joe Clark's new Progressive Conservative government waited before convening the House. In late autumn it was bringing in its first budget, and interim Liberal leader Allan MacEachen was opposing it strongly. On December 13, the Speaker of the Yukon legislature was visiting us, and I escorted him to a meeting with the Minister of National Defence, Robert Coates, whose office staff seemed very uneasy. After a very short chat, we proceeded to the Speaker's Gallery of the House of Commons, where the bells were ringing to call members to vote on the budget. The government lost, Joe Clark resigned, and the Liberals, under Trudeau *redivivus*, won the ensuing election.

A Place *at the* Table

THE DEPARTMENT OF EXTERNAL AFFAIRS posted Allan to London. Don Jamieson had been appointed as Canada's high commissioner in 1983, and Allan was to be Minister-Counsellor, Public Affairs. I planned to take a leave of absence from the House to be with him. Carleton University had allowed me to work part time on PhD course work in political science, and I would be able to finish these requirements at the London School of Economics. But I had been in London only a few days when the House invited me to compete for Principal Clerk at the Table of the House of Commons.

Flying back to Ottawa, I thought about women's pursuit of careers. Many in my generation of women hoped mainly to marry and have children. I remembered all the excitement surrounding Betty Friedan's *The Feminine Mystique* (1963). I had come late to the job market, and this was an opportunity I really couldn't miss, despite the glories of London.

Mary Anne Griffith and I won the posts — the first women to occupy a place at the Table in the House of Commons — to advise the Speaker and MPs on both sides of the House and to prepare rulings on points of order and questions of privilege for the Speaker.

From 1983, when Jeanne Sauvé was Speaker, until my departure in 1989, we started our days with the Speaker's briefings and then the Speaker's Parade down the Hall of Honour into the chamber. Allan and I spoke on the phone daily (Bell was the winner here). Each time the House adjourned for any length of time I flew to London. One weekend I travelled to Oxford University to present a paper on Standing and Special Committees of the Canadian House. Another time, while attached to the British House, I spent special time with their committees. Later the *Canadian Parliamentary Review* published a few short articles I wrote on this and related subjects.

Recognizing Names *and* Faces

MY GREATEST TEST AS PRINCIPAL CLERK came early in my tenure. Brian Mulroney's Progressive Conservatives won the September 1984 election, trouncing the Liberals under John Turner, who had just replaced Pierre Trudeau. The new prime minister knew from Joe Clark's experience that he must meet the House as soon as possible.

As the Clerk swore in each MP privately (and there were many new ones!), I watched and studied; as well, I could scour a booklet from the House's Security Service with pictures of all the members. The CBC interviewed me a few days before the opening of Parliament, and the evening news showed me preparing diligently.

As it happened, a call to vote came on the first full sitting day. John Holtby, former First Assistant Clerk of the Ontario legislature, reported in the *Globe and Mail*:

> *By demanding a recorded vote on a motion to put the House of Commons to work a day early after its three-month absence, [NDP House Leader Nelson] Riis brought onto centre stage Norah [sic] Lever, a longtime toiler on Parliament Hill.*
>
> *When the House votes, MPs stand one by one to indicate their support or disapproval of the question. First those in favour, then those opposed. Ms Lever's function is to visually recognize each MP, calling his or her name to the Clerk of the House to record the vote. Some members are situated almost half a football field away. There are 295 faces, almost 150 of them brand new, all sitting*

in places different from the last House. There is no time to look at crib notes. The task is formidable.

Of the new members, Ms Lever will have met only a few. But during the election period she had been looking at photographs of candidates, matching names, constituencies and faces. The final house seating plan was made only a few days ago. And pictures are only a partial aid. A new MP decides on a new hairstyle, a beard disappears. Eyeglasses are removed for contact lenses, thus rendering the passport-type photograph useless.

The pressure is on the calling Clerk to complete the first vote of the new Parliament error-free. She knows that every new MP is a star at home and it could harm the reputation of any new member who is reduced to "what's his name" on the coast-to-coast parliamentary television network. In the room containing the largest collection of egos in the country, being a no-name just won't do. Add to this the distraction of television and the knowledge that everyone from the Prime Minister down is riveting attention on this first vote performance. It is the ultimate test of "sang froid"…

She met it with style. Two hundred and ninety-five faces and names without error. It's an act worth catching whenever the House of Commons votes. And admission is free.

The Kingdom *of* Saudi Arabia

IN 1989 ANOTHER NEW OPPORTUNITY (the subject of this book) came my way. Allan had returned from London in 1985 to become director of trade with western Europe at External Affairs. In 1989, the cabinet appointed him ambassador to the Kingdom of Saudi Arabia, the Yemen Arab Republic (North Yemen), and the People's Democratic Republic of Yemen (South Yemen). This was too good for me to miss. I arranged for a two-year leave of absence from the House of Commons — it later grew to four!

We had briefings, received some language training, and, with excitement and sadness, made our good-byes to Allan's parents and our children — John, David, Gillian (Jill), and Christopher.

DIPLOMACY AND FRIENDSHIP

Their [the Bedouins'] possessions were few,
but each family was said to have brought
the wooden *mihbaj*, to prepare their coffee,
and the iron *saj*, to bake their bread.
The very sound of grinding coffee was considered
an invitation to anyone and everyone to come.
Stay, it suggested. *Seek shelter.*

— Anthony Shadid, *House of Stone: A Memoir
of Home, Family, and a Lost Middle East*
(Boston 2013), 306–7

PART ONE

The Kingdom *of* Saudi Arabia
(Autumn 1989—Spring 1990)

The Canadian embassy, Riyadh, Saudi Arabia

CHAPTER 1

The EMBASSY

ON THE MORNING OF SEPTEMBER 30, 1989, I felt the excitement of riding on a magic carpet over Arabia. Riyadh, our destination, sits in the centre of the Arabian peninsula. The plane circled above the city, vast swaths of bright lights aglow in a broad expanse of desert.

As our magic carpet touched down, I nervously arranged the long skirt I had purchased for the occasion. Over it I wore a loose-fitting, long-sleeved blouse. "I truly hope I fit into this culture, wonderfully strange to me," I thought, as I followed Allan down the steps to the tarmac.

"Welcome to the Kingdom of Saudi Arabia" were the first words we heard. David Hutchings, chief political officer at the Canadian embassy, greeted us, and then his wife, Mary, introduced herself. "And may I present," David said, "a representative of Saudi Protocol" — a dignified gentleman wearing the traditional white Saudi *thobe*, who welcomed us in a friendly manner and led us to a lounge, where we sat in large chairs that circled a room decorated with handsome oriental carpets. We received our first cup of coffee Saudi style — small cups of liquid with a strong flavour of cardamom.

"Remember," Allan whispered, "you should drink three cups of this coffee to honour the hospitality offered, and just wiggle your cup gently back and forth to indicate when you are finished."

Canada's official residence is attached to the embassy office (the chancery) in Riyadh's Diplomatic Quarter — a beautifully laid-out neighbourhood housing embassies and residences from all parts of the world. Palm trees line winding roads that lead to beautiful buildings.

Entering the Canadian residence

A mall, al-Kindi Plaza (1986), Diplomatic Quarter, Riyadh.
The Kingdom started building the Quarter about 1980, as it
transferred foreign embassies from Jeddah.

Sculptures of Canada geese at entrance
to Canadian official residence

The Household Staff

STANDING IN THE RESIDENCE DOORWAY when we first arrived were the household staffers I would learn to admire so much: Ali (the chief), Hanif, and Zafar — all long-time employees of the Canadian ambassador, with families back home in Pakistan. The leader of the group was Ali — hence our son David's reference to 'the A-team.' (As a youngster, David had watched a TV action-adventure series of that name, in the 1980s.) Ali performed as a sort of combined butler and cleaner. Best of all, he could set the most beautiful tables with fine linens, flowers, candles, crystal, silver, and china. Ali used a measuring device to be sure that every item was properly placed!

It was Zafar's superb laundering skills that made the linens so crisp and clean. He helped with the cleaning as well.

Hanif was the cook. Each week he would come to my office to discuss menus and presentations. Over the years he had collected many cookbooks. I confessed to him that I needed to have coloured pictures to help me make choices; he complied by offering numerous colourful copies of the *Australian Weekly Magazine*. Together we developed a very compatible and mutually respectful relationship. It worked well.

The A-team: Ali, Zafar, and Hanif

WOMEN ARE NOT ALLOWED TO DRIVE in the Kingdom of Saudi Arabia. I must admit that it really wasn't a hardship for me to be driven! The embassy provided a car and driver for the ambassador, and a pool of the same on call for the use of embassy staff members and their spouses.

Atta was the driver assigned to Allan. He was Eritrean, small in stature, and filled with kindness and goodwill. His hours were terrible because of the calls Allan made to government officials at all hours of day or night and the many receptions and events we both attended either separately or together.

An evening could be complicated. If Allan and I were invited to a Saudi home, we might have dinner in separate buildings for the men and the women. Sometimes the men's dinner finished before the women's. Atta might drive Allan home, then return to wait patiently with the other drivers for us women to depart.

When Atta drove me to the market (*souk*), he dropped me off, then left to park the car. I wandered through the crowded alleyways, and soon became conscious of the fact that Atta had come back and was with me. I appreciated his comforting presence, and was pleased occasionally to ask him to provide translation for me.

Atta was a devout Muslim and believed that it was his obligation to send back to his family in Eritrea ten per cent of his earnings, even though he had a wife and three children to care for in Riyadh. We took some comfort in knowing that he, as well as the long-serving household staff members, were reasonably paid and would receive Canadian pensions when they retired. These would be a huge help when these men returned to their families in low-income countries.

Atta and Allan

Happily in the garden

A Secure Oasis

O UR NEW HOME BASE in this fascinating, perplexing country quickly proved idyllic. On October 3, I reported to Allan's parents:

> *We have been here only three days, and each one seems packed with several days' worth of activities. The weather is beautiful! Bright and pleasant in the morning, increasingly warm and sunny throughout the day, very agreeable for sitting in the garden between 3:00 and 5:00 o'clock (and on into the evening, I suppose, although we haven't had a chance to do that yet). The garden is lovely with grass, a trellis with bougainvillea, palm trees, yellow mums and an array of pink and red flowers.*

The residence garden

Wrestling *with the* Abaya

WHEN DAVID AND MARY HUTCHINGS greeted us at the airport, Mary had come prepared. She handed me an *abaya* — a long, black, silk-like cloak to wear over my dress as I prepared to leave the airport. For the next four years this would be my uniform, which I wore everywhere outside of private homes.

Early on I wrote an article for the Canadian foreign-service magazine, *Liaison*.*

> *I'm perplexed about the use of the abaya. I'm not sure what it means to the Saudi women, or how they feel about it. I'm not sure what the Saudis expect of foreign women, nor how I, or other foreigners, should feel about it.*
>
> *Before coming to the Kingdom, I was aware that women wear the long black cloak called the abaya and black material covering their hair. I had seen only a few pictures of women wearing a veil across their faces with eyes exposed. Pictures of women with the black veil completely covering their heads are rare.*
>
> *Before my arrival here, too, I had read that urban women were more inclined to cover themselves at the behest of their husbands then were rural women. I speculated at the time, that the work of the rural women would prevent their wearing voluminous materials, which would just be in the way. Perhaps, too, there is less need for rural women to be protected from public stress in rural areas where strangers seldom visit.*
>
> *My understanding of the situation for urban women is this. In the past the veil was not as important as it is today.*

*"'Sporting' the Abaya in Saudi Arabia," *Liaison* 6, no. 6 (April 1990), 16—17.

Before the oil boom, the central area of Saudi Arabia had a small population of Bedouin tribes and villages seldom disturbed by foreigners. With the arrival of strangers from many countries, thought had to be given to protecting the Saudi culture, particularly as the country grew wealthy and major changes took place with the construction of roads, communications systems and grand new buildings. Saudi leaders had to be careful that traditional values were not set aside in the headlong rush toward modernization ...

On my first arrival in Riyadh, I wondered what I should do. I knew we would be met by a representative of the Foreign Ministry Protocol and I was anxious not to offend. Since that time I have undergone a number of differing feelings about the custom as it may, or may not apply to me. My initial, and perhaps strongest feeling is that I would like to conform as a courtesy. I am a guest in this country and I would like to behave in a manner pleasing to my hosts — and hostesses.

However, there have been times when I have felt somewhat differently. I can't forget that the wearing of this outfit is linked with a number of constraints. For example, women are not allowed to drive and, when leaving their homes, they are expected to be in the company of another woman, a son, or husband ...

So the questions remain: As more and more Saudi women are educated, will they still be supportive of wearing an abaya? Is it important for the Saudis that foreign women cover up too so that their people won't be overly influenced by a foreign culture? Is it necessary for a foreigner to conform?

Sporting my abaya

THE MAGAZINE'S EDITORIAL COMMITTEE added: "In the Foreign Service we often encounter different and to some perhaps distressing local customs, practises and laws. We can accept some of these local practises in the context of cultural sovereignty. Others are perceived as abuses of human rights. How does the abaya and what it represents fit into the picture? Nora Lever voices her own dilemma about women in Saudi society sincerely and candidly. We would be most interested to hear from her at the end of her posting to learn if she has answered her own questions about the abaya, or if they remain unresolved."

During the buildup to the Gulf War, I found it essential for me to wear the abaya. The religious police, reflecting (or leading the way) in resentment of foreign troops on Saudi soil, became increasingly officious in enforcing the tradition.

Reaching Out

IN OUR FIRST WEEKS IN RIYADH, as I wrote to his parents on November 26, Allan made a number of courtesy calls to various diplomats — a prelude to a career first for him: presenting his credentials as ambassador to the host country's head of state:

Here's another short letter to try to make sense of what we're doing! Protocol requires that the newly arrived Ambassador call on a number of people as soon as possible after arriving in the capital.

He begins his courtesy calls by visiting the Dean of the Diplomatic Corps and other ambassadors whose countries have links with ours: OECD countries, the Commonwealth, etc. Also he wants to call on several ambassadors from Middle Eastern countries. These meetings can begin before the ambassador presents his credentials to the Head of State. Diplomats who have been here a long time can advise their new colleague, filling him in on customs, politics, and personalities. It's a good learning exercise before contacts are made with ministers and departmental officials.

Here in Riyadh, Allan called on Prince Saud Al-Faisal, Foreign Minister, as a prelude to a later meeting to present his credentials to the Custodian of the Two Holy Mosques, King Fahd.

Allan sips cardamom coffee with diplomats from Gulf states during courtesy calls, before he presented his credentials.

King Fahd Door, Al-Masjid an-Nabawī (Prophet's Mosque),
in Medina, second holiest site in Islam after Al-Masjid
al-Hartām (Sacred Mosque) in Mecca. King Fahd took
the ancient style "Custodian of the Two Holy Mosques"
in 1986 and greatly expanded the Prophet's Mosque.

CHAPTER 2

The CUSTODIAN *of the* TWO HOLY MOSQUES

The Royal Court *in* Jeddah

BEFORE THEY CAN CONDUCT OFFICIAL BUSINESS with the host government, new ambassadors must present their credentials to the head of state. The Custodian of the Two Holy Mosques was King Fahd bin [son of] Abdulaziz al Saud [of the house of Saud]. Allan finally received his invitation to meet the sovereign in Jeddah, at the peripatetic Royal Court, which — with top ministers and officials — can sit also in nearby Mecca, Medina, and Taif, and of course in the capital, Riyadh.

We had learned by this time that Saudi names tell you about their bearers' lineage, their place in the scheme of things. The King's father, Abdulaziz (or Ibn Saud), had in the 1920s conquered his tribal foes in what is now Riyadh province and by 1932 ruled virtually the entire Arabian peninsula. During his long reign (1932—53), he had had many wives, and he was thought to have nearly 40 children. His favourite wife came from the powerful

Sudairi clan — Hassa bint [daughter of] Ahmad Al Sudairi. To-gether they produced seven sons (the Sudairi Seven). Since the king's death, the leadership had by 1989 passed to two of those seven. So King Fahd's name is Fahd bin Abdulaziz al Saud ("bint" would refer to a daughter).

Allan flew to Jeddah, in the west of the country on the Red Sea. This large city, with an international airport, serves as the 'gateway' for pilgrims to the holy cities of Mecca and Medina. Allan attended King Fahd in his Royal Palace by the sea. Foreign Minister Prince Saud al Faisal (the King's nephew) was there as well. After the formal presentation of documents from our sover-eign, Her Majesty Queen Elizabeth II, Allan had an opportunity to engage in conversation with the King. He leapt at the chance to raise an issue of importance to him.

An excellent exhibition — "The Kingdom Yesterday and Today" — had travelled to the United Kingdom and to the United States. In-formally, at various receptions since his arrival in Riyadh, Allan had tried to arrange for it to visit Canada, but officials had told him that it was impossible. When he had this opportunity to speak to the Custodian of the Two Holy Mosques about his suggestion, the King said, "It shall be done."

Returning to Riyadh next day, Allan received a call from the governor of Riyadh, Prince Salman bin Abdulaziz al Saud, yet an-other of the Sudairi Seven (sons of Ibn Saud) and head of the organization responsible for the exhibit. He said they would be pleased to send it to Canada. King Fahd had been a man of his word! Canadians in Montreal and Toronto would be able to see an excellent display, and Allan would enjoy increasingly good re-lations with the higher levels of the Saudi government.

Meanwhile, I too was meeting lots of interesting people. One of the experiences that seemed strange to me was being introduced always as "the wife of ... " Introductions would take place wherever we went, as people presented "His Excellency Allan Lever, Canadian Ambassador to the Kingdom of Saudi Arabia, and his wife ..." Hmmmm. Well. OK ... After an adult life of feminism, I had to gulp.

Minister of Foreign Affairs Prince Saud al Faisal
introduces Allan to the Custodian
of the Two Holy Mosques, King Fahd.

Yemen Times Two

THE COUNTRY WE KNOW TODAY as Yemen consists of the former Yemen Arab Republic (North Yemen) and the former People's Democratic Republic of Yemen (South Yemen, formerly Aden). In October 1989, Allan presented his credentials in South Yemen with little difficulty. While in the capital and port city of Aden, he had a worthwhile visit with the British representative stationed there.

Presenting his *bona fides* in North Yemen proved more difficult. The government invited us to Sana'a as its guests, which placed us on December 19 in an old hotel, unheated in cold weather. The ceremony was to take place that evening. At first, we cheered our good luck — we planned to leave Saudi Arabia on December 22 to return to Canada for Christmas.

Ha! There we were. No ceremony emerging through the foggy chill of winter. Allan called down to the hotel staff for electric heaters, and we walked briskly through the streets of Sana'a try-

Sana'a, Yemen

ing to keep warm.

Along those old streets were souks selling clothing, jackets, knives, turbans, blue plastic bags — and *qat* (the leaves of an Arabian plant that is chewed as a stimulant). Countless individuals lay in the doorways of their tiny stores, relaxed to the extreme by their constant chewing. This is a habit of a large number of Yemenis. In fact, during later visits, Allan was invited to participate along with businessmen and government officials in the private qat rooms of their homes.

Suffering in our cold, old hotel, Allan made call after call to the offices of President Ali Salah. December 20, December 21, December 22! Finally we got the word. A car would pick us up and deliver us to the palace for the big moment.

We made it just in time for the Saudia Airlines flight to Jeddah and then to New York, connecting on to Toronto. 23 hours in all. It was worth it — we had arranged for a large cottage south of Orillia, and the family awaited us.

Marketplace in Sana'a

Royal Portraits

ONE EVENING IN JUNE 1990, in Riyadh, we had visited an exhibition of portraits by Andrew Vicari, who was born in Wales to Italian parents. Vicari had invited us — insisted that we visit — after we met him at a reception a few weeks earlier and again at a piano recital at our friends Nasser and Mouna Al-Rashids' home. The exhibition was in the main foyer of the office of the Al-Rashid engineering firm in Al Dabab Street. Nasser, who was very close to the Saudi kings and advised them on the construction of all their palaces in Saudi Arabia and elsewhere, had commissioned the canvases.

The exhibition featured huge oil paintings of King Fahd and — amazing for Saudi Arabia — a few drawings of his face. Two men had encouraged Vicari to paint Saudi Arabian subjects: Sheikh Mohammad Albalkhail, the long-serving former minister of finance and economy, and later Prince Khalid, the late King Faisal's son. Vicari said, "The Saudi leaders took the initiative to allow the development of pictorial art in countries otherwise ruled by the precepts of the Koran, of which they are the guardians. They were able to interpret with insight the spirit of Mohammed who wanted to save believers from idolatry, but without prohibiting — as always had been believed previously — the representation of the human form."

Dr Ghazi Algosaibi, a poet and Saudi minister of health, has said, "Andrew Vicari has been one of the few non-Saudis to be able to cut through platitudes and frozen images and touch the soul of Arabia. The encounter of the two has done both a great service: Saudi Arabia gained an intelligent and creative artist; Andrew met his most inspiring subject. The results are gratifying to art lovers everywhere."

In 1978 he completed one of the largest, most challenging commissions ever, according to Daniel Curzi of *Figaro* — a series of 60 paintings for the royal palaces and Riyadh's King Faisal Cen-

ter for Research and Islamic Studies. For Al-Rashid, he painted ten larger-than-life portraits of King Fahd:
- the five Saudi kings to 1978 (Ibn Saud and his sons Saud, Faisal, Khalid, and Fahd) and Crown Prince Abdullah
- the commemoration of the unification of the kingdom
- the acclamation
- the man of the desert
- the man of destiny
- the custodian of a nation
- the prayer for the kingdom
- the leader and the educator
- the peacemaker
- the father of the modern kingdom

It was a captivating exhibition. Vicari's rich colours, particularly the vivid blues, are gorgeous. The brilliance of a dazzling sun in most of the pictures serves as a unifying motif throughout. Imagine Nasser Al-Rashid presenting such a gift to the Custodian of the Two Holy Mosques!

Nora and Allan with Andrew Vicari at his art exhibition

CHAPTER 3

The WORK BEGINS

Busy 'Wife *of* ... '

NO KIDDING. THIS IS WORK. Information is invaluable to every governmental representative abroad, and where better for an ambassador to dig it up than at receptions and dinners? As the 'wife of ... ,' I would not only keep my eyes and ears open on behalf of my husband, but also learn a great deal about the many languages, cultures, faiths, peoples represented in the Saudi capital. What an incredible treat!

One day, for example, I attended a delightful farewell tea for Amal Naser (who was posted to Los Angeles) and Salma Al Hassan (who was returning to Lebanon) given by one of my favourite people in Riyadh — Mrs Masarrat Jehan Khaishgi, wife of the Pakistani ambassador. She has a very sweet daughter who has recently graduated, plans to marry in September, and hopes to be able to move to Ottawa with her husband. She is planning to undertake graduate work at Carleton University.

Before Our Very Eyes

O NE EVENING WE HAD DINNER at the Japanese residence. The ambassador and his wife were both charming people with many years' experience in the diplomatic service. She was attractive, beautifully dressed, and very genteel. When she first arrived in Riyadh, she told me, she had been somewhat shy and had a fair amount of difficulty speaking English. A previous posting had been in Paris, and she said she felt a bit more comfortable in French. If I recall correctly, our first conversation together (when she paid a courtesy call on me earlier) was a comfortable chat in French, and when she sent me a thank-you note after a dinner here it was in French. However, English is used in diplomatic circles here much more than French, and she quickly improved a great deal.

The guests that evening were the Italian ambassador, Mario Maiolini, and his wife, Vivi, and the Australian ambassador's wife, so the language that the hosts and guests had in common seemed to be English (lucky us!).

During dinner our host pointed to a poem he had written in Japanese characters and hung in the dining area. Laughing at his intended humour, he said, "I had experienced the void of the desert surrounding Riyadh and found it brilliant with the colour of the golden (sunshine), thus coming to the conclusion that void was indeed colour and vice versa."

This pithy poetry provoked much philosophical conversation. The Italian ambassador tended to preach a bit, but the evening was fun and allowed me also to take in the architectural beauty of the Japanese residence: huge open spaces, simple, tastefully decorated — it's really wonderful to see.

The ambassador explained to us, at a counter where the food was being cooked in front of us, what we were eating and how to eat it. The menu was as follows: *tsukidashi* (quenelle of fish, etc.); *ae-mono* (spinach); *sunomono* (abalone, cucumber, and seaweed with vinegar); *tempura* (shrimps, fish, cuttlefish, and vegetables); fried rice; and *miso* (soup). I peeked over at Allan to see how he was doing, and he was savouring the novel delicacies. He loved all of it as much as I did. It was delicious, and the tiny portions of food were very attractive. Dessert was served in an adjacent room, where, having removed our shoes before entering, we sat on cushions on the floor.

Trial Run

ONE DAY, THE AMBASSADOR of the Federal Republic of Germany and Mrs Wolfgang Bente (Suzanne — she's French) held a reception to bid farewell to Mr and Mrs Bernd Erbel, whom they were replacing. Suzanne said it was a sort of trial run, since it was their first party in Riyadh. Their residence is lovely, with a beautiful garden surrounding it. Inside the ceilings are high, and the decor is very simple. Suzanne prefers more cosyness, but I liked the place very much.

At the party I talked with Abdul Karim H. Alyusuf, project manager for Saudi Hotels and Resort Areas Co. I expressed an interest in travelling to Abha and Al-Baha, inland from the Red Sea. He urged me to be in touch with him whenever we planned to go. He said he would like to be helpful. His company also has a hotel in Tabuk, in northwestern Saudi Arabia. I told him that I had been wanting to go there, rent a car, and travel to nearby Aqaba, in Jordan, and possibly other parts of that kingdom. He was very pleasant; I wanted to keep in touch with him. I met his wife later. She was following a social sciences course at university, with a couple more years to go. She had just finished a final exam.

The A-Team in Action

O UR TURN. WE HAD A GREAT DINNER THE NEXT NIGHT. We used the long table in the dining-room for the 20 guests. (Ali says round tables look like a restaurant! I would argue with him. I think they are very useful for promoting a less formal type of atmosphere. Also, it's easier to place people at round tables without having to place them at the end — below the salt, as it were.)

Anyway, the dining-room looked beautiful. The long table gleamed: Zafar had ironed the linen placemats beautifully; pink and white flowers graced five small silver containers, with a slightly larger one in the centre. Silver candelabras with long white candles (very hard to find here, so we bring them from Canada or London) added the final touch.

Dinner at the residence with our 20 guests

The food seemed just right. I received a phone call the next morning from Vivi Maiolini, who raved about the dinner. In the car on the way home, she told me, she and Mario had discussed how great the *dacquoise* dessert was. I thought I must tell Hanif, the cook. (Vivi also wanted to play tennis and start to play bridge again. I was keen to do both those things too, but am reluctant to tie myself down to specific dates and times. At the time both Allan and I were trying to make it through all the engagements we had scheduled to the end of the month.)

Our guests were interesting. We had met D. Osman Alfuragh (also Alfraigh or Alfraih) and his German wife, Burgi, at the home of his uncle, Mohammed Alfuragh. He's a nephrologist who trained in Germany and very pleasant to talk to. Also very nice are Kay Alaskary (American) and her husband, Alaudeen, chief of communications in the Ministry of Foreign Affairs.

Mouna's 'Salon'

ALLAN WAS SAYING DURING LUNCH ONE DAY that the recital we attended at Mouna Al-Rashid's home the previous week was probably an event we'll always remember. The 'salon' was so lavishly decorated with candelabras and flowers, and the little girls were so elaborately dressed for the occasion! Three or four of them were really beautiful and even more attractive (in a weird sort of way) because their hair was coiffed and adorned with sparkles and they wore very tasteful makeup (by grown-up standards). Saudi women's mastery of eye makeup renders them particularly lovely. And it's no wonder that the men insist on covering them up — they are a treasure to keep hidden! But it is surprising to see eleven-year-olds looking so provocative.

Meech Lake!

O NE MORNING IN LATE JUNE 1990, as he joined me for coffee and toast, Allan inquired, "What's happening in Canada this morning?"

"Newspapers today," I reported, "are still including items about Canada's [Meech Lake] constitutional crisis. Even though the first ministers have reached agreement, the legislatures in Manitoba, New Brunswick, and Newfoundland must still ratify the accord."

"New Brunswick has done so," Allan replied, "but there is a hold-up in Manitoba, where an Aboriginal NDP member is refusing to give the necessary unanimous consent to have the motion debated immediately without the usual two days' notice. He will likely withhold his consent throughout the whole process, slowing things up considerably. He has the support of the Aboriginal people all over Canada; they feel left out of the process."

In the meantime, we speculate, the Newfoundland legislature must be considering what to do. Liberal Premier Clyde Wells still complains about the meetings behind closed doors, which took place in Ottawa the previous week, and accuses Prime Minister Mulroney of deliberately gambling with the nation's future by leaving negotiations till the last minute.

This is all we know from the news we receive here — short articles in the local English-language press and a fax from the *Globe and Mail* five days a week. The fax that David sent to us from his office at McCarthy Tétrault law firm in downtown Toronto last night at 10:20 was marvellous — he had pasted together clippings from newspapers (*Globe and Mail* and *Toronto Star*). We were feeling starved for information about the great debate, so were very glad to receive the up-to-date information. Allan distributed photocopies around the office immediately.

English *v.* Arabic

W̲E RECEIVE THREE ENGLISH-LANGUAGE Saudi newspapers each day with our breakfast at 7:30 a.m. Surprising, since it's a local paper, the *Riyadh Daily* is our favourite. It includes articles about businessmen, diplomatic occasions and meetings with the various ministries, religion (a crucial topic here), travel, medicine and fitness, and international news. The *Arab News* and the *Gazette* are also interesting. By the time you read the third paper, however, you can skim through it, because most of the news is the same.

All the national political, regulatory, and decision-making items are written by the government-controlled Saudi Press Agency (SPA). Knowing that, we still find it useful to become familiar with what is, in fact, the government line. But I can't help feeling enveloped in a sort of fog, because there is no criticism of the prevailing authorities. Seemingly, the country has no crime and no dissatisfaction with the regime. We read about a special program to combat drugs; we know that executions take place in the public square every few weeks — beheadings, mostly of drug dealers, sometimes of 'highway robbers.' But the news published for public consumption is only positive on the national front.

So the focus of the news is much different in Saudi Arabia than in Canada. To be sure not to miss what the Arabic-language press is reporting, Allan has recently started receiving a daily analysis of the Arab newspapers from the translator in the office. So far, I do not detect any significant difference in emphasis or analysis in the domestic reporting of the two languages.

PART TWO

Jeddah *and* Yemen
(Summer 1990)

CHAPTER 4

Hajj WEDDINGS *in* JEDDAH

Monday, June 18, 1990

TOMORROW AFTERNOON I will be going to a surprise baby shower for Pam Saunders, secretary at our embassy. Bernadette Bollman, who arrived back in the Kingdom a few days ago, is having the gang from the office (Ron Bollman is trade counsellor). It will be a sort of 'farewell' too, since Pam and Colin Suter are planning to leave for London on September 3rd.

But this morning I played tennis with Deirdre McGoldrick (Australia), Rose Ali (Singapore), and Christina Harttila (Finland). We used the court at the Rezayyat (air-conditioned) Ladies' Fitness Center.

The main topic of conversation before and after the game was the wedding (*nikah*) of the King's wife's sister. Invitations arrived only yesterday (Sunday), and the wedding reception is to take place in the Royal Palace in Jeddah on Thursday! This is the season of the *hajj* (the annual pilgrimage to Mecca — this year: June 23—July 1), and the city's airports and hotels are full of pilgrims on their way to Mecca and Medina. Christina has been suggesting that, if enough ambassadors' wives intend to attend the wedding, perhaps Royal Protocol might arrange for a plane to go and return the same day. In my case, other arrangements are in the works.

Allan may be able to arrange appointments with some ministers and officials he needs to see. (Most of the ministries' higher authorities are in Jeddah these days because the Custodian of the Two Holy Mosques is holding court there.) If the meetings and the flight reservations materialize, Allan and I will go to Jeddah together.

To further complicate matters, I have another invitation to a wedding reception in Jeddah, next Sunday! The bride is the daughter of Amal Madani, whose husband, Nizar, runs the Western Europe and North America division of the Saudi Ministry of Foreign Affairs, central to Allan's work. He is also very hard to attract to events at the embassy or residence. Amal herself will not attend mixed gatherings, but I see her frequently at women's luncheons and teas. I basically have to go to Jeddah to attend both weddings.

If only this were not the busy month around the hajj! I would love to have asked Atta to drive us to Jeddah. We could have attended the first wedding on Thursday, spent a couple of days sight-seeing by driving to Taif, and then returned for the Sunday wedding. However, everyone agrees that it is not wise to drive to and from Jeddah these days. Even Atta, who loves Jeddah and would welcome the opportunity to go there, says this isn't a good time for such a trip.

Street scene in Jeddah's historic Al-Balad

Tuesday, June 26, 1990

WE'VE JUST RETURNED FROM JEDDAH. While we were away, Meech Lake failed and Jean Chrétien was elected leader of the Liberal party. But Canada is far away.

We had travelled to Jeddah to attend the two weddings — the first (on Thursday) at the palace given by one of King Fahd's wives for her sister, the other (on Sunday) in Lailati Hall in honour of Noha Madani.

I was curious to see the King's palace and to experience a reception there. I never seem to learn that a Saudi invitation for 9 p.m. actually beckons the guests for much later. I arrived about 9:45 — still much too early.

The Royal Palace stands on a natural island supplemented by much reclaimed land along the Corniche on the Red Sea. On the water is a huge waterspout, which is floodlit at night when the Custodian of the Two Holy Mosques (King Fahd) is in residence. Driving along a causeway, we entered through a series of three gates. Palm trees lined boulevards that led to the reception hall. Security guards along the route were courteous and caused no delay.

After Allan and the driver left me at the entrance to a great hall, I peered inside to see six long rows of chairs with 30 to 40 seats on each side of a central aisle, which boasted round tables covered with gilt-threaded table cloths and baskets of candies. I could see young women dancing in this central aisle. At the far end of the room there was a raised dais for the bride when she (finally!) appeared.

"Nora — over here," sang Sooja, wife of H.E. Pyung Kug Choo of South Korea. Most of the ambassadors' wives were already sitting in the third row on the far side. (The large over-stuffed armchairs in the first and second rows swallowed up dozens of women who were relatives of both bride and groom.) I was glad to see Sooja.

She glowed in her pale turquoise national dress and was next to the wife of Japan's consul-general, whose crisply starched national dress radiated sunshine yellow. Other countries represented included Algeria, Bangladesh, Ghana, Italy, Pakistan, Singapore, Sudan, and Tunisia. Soon the group staying at the U.S. consulate came in: Inge Berghs (Belgium), Pat Freeman (U.S.), Juliette Hakizimana (Burundi), Christina Harttila (Finland), and Fatima Oleson (Denmark). Smartest of all was Dorly de Ocerin (Spain), who arrived close to midnight. The bride finally appeared about 1 a.m.

A long evening. Loud music pre-empted attempts at conversation. I tried to remember little tidbits of conversation for use in the few seconds between songs. Finally, however, resignation set in, and the row of ambassadors' wives peered curiously at the people sitting across the way. They, of course, were doing the same thing. The older women, dressed in black, with henna-black hair parted in the middle and pulled severely close to their head, sat in the front seats, along with the more elegant princesses of high station. Sitting in front of us was the wife of Prince Salman, no. 4 in the Saudi hierarchy. She was ravishing in a white dress adorned with sparkling diamonds. Other women were dressed in bright oranges and yellows, and burgundies, with lots of flowers and sequins.

At 1 a.m., dancing guests melted away to allow four little girls and the bride to sway down the centre aisle. A woman from Royal Protocol fussed over them. Other women competed, fixing the bride's gown, adjusting the train.

"They need a stage manager," I whispered to Sooja. The King did not allow the groom to join the women. In this regard, practice seems to be mixed in Saudi Arabia. Sometimes, the groom's father escorts his son down the lengthy central corridor to join the bride on the dais. Then the father retires (happily, no doubt) to leave his son in the room filled with hundreds of women. In this case, the bride left the room after an hour or two, to join the groom in an adjacent chamber. Later we were invited to yet another hall for a buffet dinner. Back to the hotel around 3:45 a.m.

But the other wedding in Jeddah was a different story! Amal Madani's daughter was marrying her cousin, and the groom's sister (also Amal's niece) was marrying too. The two couples in the invitation were (1) Nizar Madani's daughter, Noha, and Arab Hashem's son, Waleed; and (2) Salem Kayyal's son, Khaled, and Arab Hashem's daughter, Amal. During the long evening I finally figured out that Mrs Arab Hashem was the mother of a bride and a groom.

A big surprise when I entered Lailati Hall — this time around 11:30 p.m. for a 10-o'clock invitation — still too early! Round tables with about twelve seats at each filled a huge hall. There were hundreds of women there, everyone having a great time. Arabic music murmured in the background, allowing animated conversation. The volume would climb higher and higher, but for now we could chat away in eager anticipation.

As my eyes alighted on a large stage, I saw two women in traditional wedding gowns from the Medina area. Those old costumes held elaborate embroidery with gold threads on bright pink material. I could imagine that the gowns were so heavy those brides of old couldn't move without help. Joining them for a while was a lovely young woman in a modern white wedding gown, which she had worn at her own nuptials a week earlier. Some elegant couches and flower arrangements completed the furnishing of the stage, but leaving lots of room for dancing.

Drums pounded their beat, throats of Arab singers projecting sounds surreal. Dozens of slender women snaked their way across the stage. Everyone was having fun! I have never enjoyed so much the rhythm of the Arabic music. Graceful young women performed as individuals, but seemed to link with others for a

few moments as they moved about the stage. Even Amal Madani, who is one of the most conservative women I have met — no
mixed parties, and head covered at our house with its male staff
— danced and moved her hips in a most provocative way.

The lights in the hall dimmed. Dramatic music rose in a cre-
scendo of anticipation. Spotlights cast arcs across the wall and
ceiling, finally coming to rest on a balcony at the end of the room
opposite the stage. Several minutes of anticipation ... Then one
couple, Amal and Khaled, appeared. They stood on the balcony,
throwing rose petals down to the women below. Five minutes
later they withdrew, came downstairs, and entered the hall, making their way to the stage. I saw that the colourful array of ladies'
costumes had turned to mostly black, covering heads, faces, and
any bare arms in the presence of a man.

The bride's mother invited a few close relatives to come forward to greet the bride and groom. Later, when Noha and Waleed
came to the stage, we diplomatic gals sashayed forth to greet the
bride. During the few minutes that Waleed spent on stage, mother Amal and a few young relatives danced. Never have I seen a
man with eyes cast down so discreetly! When both men had left
the hall, lots of women joined the dancers on the stage.

About 3 a.m. the men returned for the buffet dinner. It was delicious (much better food than the old King had served). I helped myself at a table of Chinese food and sat at a table with Amy from Taiwan, Mrs Khaishgi from Pakistan (my favourite ambassador's wife),
Leyla Shura and her daughter, Amal Nazer (who is leaving right after
Eid al-Adha for the posting in Los Angeles), and Abla Mashaat.

Back to the hotel at 4:30 a.m.

"I certainly don't keep these hours in Canada!" I exclaimed to
the receptionist as I retrieved my key. When I found our room,
Allan was, of course, sound asleep in bed.

Al-Balad (The Town/City), the formerly walled, historic area
of Jeddah, now a UNESCO World Heritage Site

Above, in Al-Balad, Jeddah: a doorway (left) and Bab Makkah (Mecca Gate) souk; below, in Jeddah: Abdul Raouf Khalif Mosque and Museum.

Sana'a, capital of Yemen. The old walled city
is a UNESCO World Heritage Site.

CHAPTER 5

YEMEN: *From* SANA'A *down to* ADEN

Thursday, July 5, 1990

WE'VE JUST RETURNED from a marvellous trip in the newly unified country of Yemen. Allan is responsible for representing Canada in what became one country in June of this year. The capital is in Sana'a, old capital of North Yemen. From now on, Allan will probably direct a lot of his attention there. Ministers he had met in Aden (capital of South Yemen) are moving north to their new capital. Major oil exploration is continuing in the south, however, and our embassy will no doubt keep in touch with Canadian Oxy (Canadian Occidental Petroleum) and Petrocan, which are both directing their field operations — drilling for oil — from the port of Aden.

We set out last Thursday, June 28, with Nick and Anna Cocking. Lieutenant-Colonel Nicholas Cocking, senior British military adviser to the Saudi National Guard, and his wife, Anna, had become good friends of ours. During his lengthy career with the British military service, Nick had been base commander in several countries. Anna had been 'mother' to all the military personnel under his command. In Riyadh, she adopted a similar role in relation to the diplomatic corps!

Nick had been posted with the British military in Yemen many years earlier, so was keen to make a return trip. So were all the Yemenis living and working in Saudi Arabia! It was the second-last day of the Eid al-Adha, marking the hajj. The Riyadh airport was crowded. The plane left about two hours late, overfilled with families on their way home. Children sat on the laps of parents and milled about the plane.

"Yikes! We're moving on the runway, and the front door isn't yet closed." I held my breath. Allan shared some concern about the safety of the overloaded flight, but we finally landed safe and sound in Sana'a.

We were met at the airport by our man in Sana'a, Fouad Gohairy, and by the four-wheel-drive Toyota with driver that Fouad had arranged for our trip. The driver's name was Mohammed bin Saleh. I didn't catch the name of his tribe when Fouad told us, but he was an excellent driver — fast and sure.

Although most people were preparing for the Eid al-Adha, Allan met Foreign Minister Dr Abdul Kareem Al Irina. He also had meetings with the chief of protocol and the director of the North American desk. He had lunch with a gentleman who will likely be Canada's honorary consul-general in Yemen before too long.

I visited the old city and wandered through the souk. Restoration of the lovely old mud buildings was well under way, with the help of Italy and other nations. They are several stories high, all joined together. Windows are decorated with a sort of whitewash known as alabaster. I recall reading that Yemenis customarily decorate their windows to indicate they have taken part in the hajj.

Early Saturday morning we set out from Sana'a for the villages of Shibam, Kokoban, and Thula. On the way we stopped on a hill overlooking the valley of Wadi Dhar, with its striking architecture and the historic palace of Dar al-Hajar. On the hill we found a cluster of Yemeni men. Mohammed explained that they were meeting for a wedding. As we engaged some of the men in conversation, others gathered around. Some beat drums, and they began to perform a traditional sword dance. Next thing I noticed was that Allan had been offered a knife — the traditional curved Yemeni knife they all carry — and had joined in the dancing!

The drive up to Kokoban required some courage. Steep, winding roads look over the most spectacular views. There are no guardrails, so one certainly feels vulnerable as the car careens around the mountainside. The driver was excellent, but surely the car could bounce off a rock on the road or veer to avoid an oncoming car cutting corners on the very narrow road, and tumble down the mountainside. It doesn't take too much imagination to

Sixteenth-century mud-brick towers, old walled city of Shibam, a UNESCO World Heritage Site

make you grip the sides of your seat in stark terror!

However, the scenery was wonderful. Mud and stone houses clustered in small villages nestled in the hillside. Aesthetically, these small communities are very attractive because they are made with local materials and seem to constitute an integral part of the countryside. Often you had to look closely to see them; otherwise they blended into the landscape and were simply part of a beautiful panorama.

Only when you actually drive into a village do you see how crowded, dirty, littered with garbage, paper, and plastic it is. We need not feel superior about this; within my memory, people used to throw trash out their car windows while driving along highways in southern Ontario. I believe it was only in the 1940s or 1950s that the authorities started fining people $50 for doing so. But the litter in the narrow streets and alleyways and also in the countryside of Yemen is extraordinary. Whoever manufactures pale blue, thin plastic bags and plastic bottles for drinking water should stop. It makes you think of the scandalous marketing of baby formula to developing countries, where people could ill afford to buy it and where the water is not clean enough to mix safely with powdered milk.

At Thula, a woman stopped to invite me to accompany her to her house. I followed her along a narrow alleyway as she carried a full pail of water on her head. She was dressed in a dark, dusty cloak with her head covered but face exposed. She led me into the dark entrance to her home, deposited the pail of water on a recessed ledge in the mud wall, and then proceeded up three or four flights to a small 'living-room.' I sat down with her on rugs on the floor, and she offered me some bread. She showed me how to dip the bread in sweet syrup, which had floating in it some kind of fruit, which looked like pitted cherries. We smiled

Thula mountain cityscape

at each other a lot and tried to find some words the other would understand. Finally we resorted to counting in Arabic, after having exhausted our repertoire of questions about her health and the loveliness of the morning. I was saved by the arrival of three or four children — Allan and an old fellow who was leading us around the village had told them to find us and move us along. Whew! But it really was interesting to see inside these dark old buildings and to experience a feeling of 'sisterhood' with a woman living in such penurious circumstances.

We moved along. The Toyota Landcruiser is amazingly comfortable for a long trip. There was lots of room for five people, suitcases, camera equipment, etc. The Cockings carried four different kinds of cameras! They had a video camera, which provided for voice commentary, an Olympus with zoom, etc., a Polaroid, and a disposable camera, which takes three shots at a time to produce a panorama.

The trip was planned to take two days, stopping the first night in Taiz. It was a wonderful drive between Sana'a and Taiz. At first I was surprised at the stark desolation of the bare, rocky mountains. I had always heard that Yemen, which is mostly high above sea level, was cool, lush, and green. As Nick explained with a chuckle, these descriptions are relative to what a person is familiar with. If you are comparing the countryside with the desert, I guess you might think it is verdant. Coming from Canada, one might think that's stretching things a bit.

Actually, after we had travelled for a few hours from Sana'a, the scenery had become more green. Looking down into valleys from the winding mountainside road, we could see fields of corn and other vegetables, as well as some trees and shrubs. As we drove along, it became a sort of game for us to decide whether we would really classify the growth as 'lush.' At times the most we

Typical structures, old walled city, Sana'a

Classic landscape with traditional mountain villages in Yemen

Above: The village of Al Hajjarah on Haraz mountains, Yemen
Below: Traditional architecture in mountain villages

Above: Panorama of Haid Al-Jazil in Wadi Doan Hadramaut, Yemen
Below: Yemeni mountain village

were prepared to admit was 'demi-lush.'

There were perhaps three main features we were looking for: the 'lush' vegetation; the unique architecture; and the terracing of the mountainside, so that farmers can plant their crops. Nick took plenty of pictures that captured all these interesting features, and it was a mesmerizing trip all the way.

Besides the scenery, which captivated us as we drove along in the car (or, rather, hurtled through space), we enjoyed several stops in small villages. Each time we left the car we were surrounded by eager, friendly children who loved to talk and to have their pictures taken. It was a special treat for them when Anna allowed them to look through the lens of the video camera, but it was sometimes difficult for her to escape from them when they were having so much fun.

At one village, we stopped for a half-hour while Mohammed went to a restaurant for lunch. As we wandered along a narrow street, we came upon a mosque, where a young man who identified himself as a teacher invited us to follow him. He took us up dark stairs to his living quarters. The room was surprisingly attractive, with colourful carpets and cushions and a TV set on the floor at the far end. We felt his offer of refreshment could not be politely refused, so sat with him for 15 minutes or more sipping a cinnamon-flavoured tea. (I think at that point Allan was exercising certain strength of will to keep the fluid moving in the right direction!) As we left, the chap showed us pictures of the local imam and finally made it clear to us that he would not be averse to receiving a donation on behalf of that religious leader. Allan and Nick complied.

Our hotel in Taiz was not exactly luxurious. Nick laughingly told us later he was amused at the momentary catch of breath as we all peered out the car window at our home-away-from-home.

However, it was clean (as one says with a stiff upper lip), and the food we had for supper was OK too. We charged off early next morning towards Aden.

Whereas Sana'a is on a height of land 2,300 metres above sea level, and Taiz is 1,500 metres, Aden is on the edge of the Gulf of Aden in the Arabian Sea, which is really part of the Indian Ocean. Aden is hot! The temperature was about 42 degrees Celsius, not as high as Riyadh, but very, very humid. It is interesting to find that the only way to cope is to stop fighting the discomfort. You simply relax and let the perspiration run down your body. You also drink lots of water.

To reach Aden on Canada Day, we drove along the peninsula, which surrounds a vast, natural harbour, and into the old, deteriorating former capital. We headed through city streets, along the seaside, and up the towering black mountain, which hovers over it all. The mountain is volcanic, and Nicholas explained that the district known as Crater sits in the crater of the volcano.

Maala Cemetery, along the water, was very moving. Allan sat on the Commonwealth War Graves Commission while in London in the mid-1980s, and this is one of its charges. Aden was a crucial naval base and saw heavy fighting during both world wars, and the site holds the remains, or honours the memory, of more than 300 Commonwealth service members.

We had lunch at the Golden Mohar Hotel in the old city before going to check in at the Canadian Oxy camp along the coast about three miles outside the city. There we found a cluster of trailers built by ATCO of Calgary, shipped from its plant in Saudi Arabia's Eastern Province. These structures housed the Canadians searching and drilling for oil.

Erwin Noyes and his wife, Laurie, greeted us with their usual warm hospitality, and Jennifer Topping was there too. Jennifer told us that the United Nations Development Programme has hired her permanently now, and she will go to New York to start her training early in the new year. We also met a lovely couple, Gwen and Alistair, and their three children (Paula, David, and Scott). The Noyes youngsters had grown since I had seen them the previous autumn. Graham was three and Emira probably a year old. Later in the day I delivered the toys I had brought from Riyadh.

The Cockings stayed in the Oxy guesthouse, and Allan and I with Ross Munro at the new Petrocan camp next door. Ross is a nice young man from Calgary. He told me he had been working with Petrocan for nine years; he had done a lot of travelling to various projects around the world, but this was his first opportunity to see a project through on site, and he was delighted to have the challenge. His wife is back in Calgary for the summer working on an MBA.

For both Nick and Anna, this visit to Aden was a nostalgic experience, returning after some 26 years. It was absorbing to hear from Nick about some of the military expeditions the British conducted before they pulled out in 1968. For example, he pointed to a mountaintop where terrorists had been encamped; during the night some British commandos had scaled the mountain and were lined up facing the terrorists as they awoke at dawn.

Nick was appalled at the deterioration since the time of the British Protectorate. Certainly, the last 20 years of Communist rule have done the country no good at all. While Aden historically was a major port, with dozens of ships in its harbour at any time, now it's poverty-stricken and desolate, with only a few straggling boats in sight. Buildings are broken and shabby, and litter lies everywhere. Its only redeeming features are the beautiful sea and the stark, dramatic black mountains hovering over it.

Erwin Noyes and Ross Munro jointly hosted a party that night, to celebrate Canada Day a day late and to introduce the Canadian ambassador. They had about 40 people from the various embassies that had not yet moved to Sana'a and from other camps, and projects. It was a great party. The buffet was catered by a company that provides food to the oil companies' camps in the desert, and we all understood why the men are really happy with the meals they receive. The British ambassador, Douglas Gordon, was there. (Actually, since the two Yemens have united and the capital is now Sana'a, Gordon becomes consul-general. He expects to leave for another posting in three months.) We enjoyed the evening.

Our original plan had been to fly out of Aden next morning. However, during the trip we found that Alyendi Airlines had cancelled the flight to Sana'a. So we adjusted our plans and arranged to drive back to Sana'a in time for our 2:45 p.m. flight to Riyadh. This required a 6 a.m. departure.

Mohammed, the driver, had elected to sleep on the beach

The legendary port of Aden, Yemen

across the road from the camps. He was pretty sleepy when Anna finally found him in the morning, but we managed to leave just a few minutes after six.

During the drive down to Aden, the many differing kinds of terrain we saw within only a few hours so intrigued me that I decided to keep a list of terms to describe the various landscapes. Shortly after leaving the sea at Aden, we passed through flat land with grey stone and gravel. It seemed like only a few minutes before we were looking out at sand dunes like the ones in the movie *Lawrence of Arabia*. This was followed by sandy terrain with tufts of grey bushes, which looked like tumbleweed but were firmly attached to the ground. Then barren mountains in the near and far distance, followed by sand, trees, gravel, and some more greenery near Taiz. (We reached Taiz around 8:15 a.m.)

Driving up the mountainside again we enjoyed once more the stunning view of the valley below, with the mud houses and the terraced gardens on the mountainside, as well as in the wadi below. This part may qualify as 'lush'; indeed, Allan allowed that if he ever had to live in Yemen he would settle there. Soon we were over the top and on our way down the other side of a mountain, where we saw a patchwork of fields more like those you would see in England. This is the only area we saw that looked more familiar to Western eyes.

Twenty minutes later we were travelling through barren, rocky mountains again, followed by a somewhat fertile plain. It really was astonishing to see the rapid changes of scenery.

We arrived in Sana'a in good time, bade farewell to Mohammed (who had been an excellent driver), and climbed aboard our flight. Arriving home only one hour late, we were glad to soak in the tub and enjoy the modern luxuries of Saudi Arabia ... no garbage on the streets of Riyadh!

A mosque in Taiz, Yemen

The tower-like *manāra* (literally 'lighthouse' = Eng. minaret) — here in the old walled city of Sana'a, Yemen — traditionally ventilated the mosque in a hot climate, and the *muezzin* would call the faithful to prayer (the *adhan*) from the gallery high atop the shaft. Even unamplified, the summons can travel hundreds of metres. Modern air conditioning and speaker systems have moved many muezzins down from the gallery. The muezzin from one or more of the five mosques in Riyadh's new Diplomatic Quarter would probably have been audible at the Canadian embassy when Nora and Allan Lever were there.

CHAPTER 6

MUEZZIN'S CALL

July 1990

T ONIGHT I'M GOING TO SNUGGLE in the den with a new book.
I have brought with me just a nice-sized piece of carrot cake
with yummy white icing to keep the wolf away from the door.
Glad I swam a mile this morning. (I'll gladly swim more if it becomes necessary. This food is too good to believe!)

I'm reading *Good Times*, an autobiography by Russell Banks,
an entertaining columnist with the *New York Times*. I want to cap-
ture some of the good stuff. What I'm coming to realize at such
an advanced age is that other people's autobiographies are so
interesting partly because they have experienced feelings similar
to one's own.

For example: Banks has a chapter he titles "Fathers." He seems
to be figuring out what has been perplexing me: "Rather late in
life, when my own children were grown, I became aware that
when they were growing up I had not been a very good father ...
I'd come to age in (an) astounding prosperity (the 1950's) when a

husband's role was to go to the office and become a success while the wife's job was to get the children born and smartened up for a really good college. Men from this world obviously wouldn't give fatherhood the priority, the energy, the study, and the seriousness it required."

This gets me thinking about motherhood. When friends would exclaim about how wonderful it was that I was able to look after a family as well as work and study, I had to say frankly (if not to them, at least to myself) that something had to suffer and it must be the household. I also was able to comfort myself, however, by knowing that Grandmother was there in the household. But the point I am making here is this: I miss the kids desperately; and I wonder if I missed the boat when they were younger because I spent so little time with them.

July 1990

ONE MORNING A WEEK OR TWO LATER, as I swam my daily 120 lengths of the pool, I thought of various projects for the autumn. I enjoy writing most of all, so considered several topics that might be worth pursuing.

One essay could be a profile of Indian women I have met. They strike me as being well educated and intelligent, as well as socially conscious. The wife of the Indian ambassador has hosted a stunning presentation of Indian saris; various people are using the exhibit to collect money for charitable organizations. She also invited a large group of women to her home to see and hear an explanation of her daughter's pre-nuptial ceremony prior to her wedding in India this summer. (Come to think of it, the Pakistani ambassador's wife is also very interesting; her daughter is also marrying this summer. Perhaps one could compare the customs of the two countries.) The Indian ambassador's wife has written commentaries that Saker Mistri read at both these events. Mrs Mistri, too, would make a good subject. She is a Zoroastrian — an ancient Persian religion that encourages its members to marry within the faith. There are only about 2½ million adherents; in India, co-religionist Parsis, or Parsees (Persians), number in the tens of thousands. In any event, Mrs Mistri is a very articulate woman who could give me lots of information. Another Indian woman in Riyadh whom I enjoy very much is Arouna Mehta.

Another essay could give an account of the life (and lives) of ambassadors' wives in general and specifically in Riyadh. To fill in the general picture, I would have to use Pam McDougall's exhaustive and authoritative *Report for the Royal Commission on Conditions of Foreign Service* (1981). Perhaps too I would want to check the report by Kristina (wife of Derek Fraser, Canadian ambassador to Hungary), whom I had met in Budapest in 1989, when, as a Principal Clerk in the House of Commons, I attended the Interparliamentary Union's 81st Assembly.

What about a detailed essay on Riyadh's Diplomatic Quarter? Perhaps for Tomorrow's Youth Organization's journal, *Ahlan Wa Sahlan*, or our department's *Liaison* magazine? I have done an outline by hand.

I swam along, thinking of the past. As a youngster I had spent most of my time playing the piano, practising several hours a day until finally becoming an associate of the Royal Conservatory of Toronto (ARCT) at the age of 17. I particularly enjoyed playing duets and trios at local music festivals. On several occasions Wilma Cobb and I raised the roof with our rendition of a duet of Ernest Lecuona's electrifying *Malagueña*!

And trios could be especially entertaining. We three 10-year-olds would practise our piece of music in my family's dining-room, then dial a random number on the telephone to ask the person who responded, "Would you like to hear some beautiful music?" The lucky individual always listened and then would praise our performance! How very kind of the residents of Port Colborne!

But I wondered what had been missing in my background to make me so unaware of parts of the world such as the Middle East when I was growing up and even in my adult years. I suspect I was like a lot of Canadians who are content to spend their days in North America and occasionally have a holiday in the Caribbean or Europe. My parents were quite interesting people. Mother had been well educated, graduating from the University of Toronto about 1920; she taught English at the senior levels in high school and painted in oil at the family cottage in Ontario's Kawartha Lakes during the summers. Dad had been a lawyer, finally a judge. My own aspirations were limited until a couple of years before we moved to Ottawa when I went back to school. I felt ambitious from 1970 to 1990 and had some academic and professional success. But there are so many people who have grown up with such interesting experiences! I was just catching up.

In Riyadh, the *muezzin's* call to prayer (*adhan*) five times a day, for example. How different from my experience! And what a beautiful sound, which can stay with a person for a lifetime. According to the brochure that my sister, Ruth Hutchinson, and I received, it sounds from the city's two thousand mosques, reminding its people of the call to righteousness and proper living. "An understanding of the true Saudi character begins with religious beliefs that encompass all aspects of life, from the political and legal system to personal morals and conduct."

Children and adults walking by Riyadh's Grand Mosque,
at sunset, before prayer time

PART THREE

Developing Storm

(August—November 1990)

CHAPTER 7

Saddam Invades Kuwait

(August 1990)

Friday, August 3, 1990

THE RADIO SHOUTED: Thursday, August 2, 1990: Saddam Hussein Marches on Kuwait! We were in Toronto for our son David's wedding to Siobhan Ryan. It was a joyous occasion, and they were off to the airport for a lovely wedding trip.

Hard to believe that no one realized that this crisis was likely to happen. The brutal Iraqi dictator had been making belligerent noises about disputed territory, and he had been objecting to the overproduction of oil by Kuwait and the United Arab Emirates. At a meeting of OPEC in Geneva, the offending oil states had agreed to keep their production within the approved limits, which seemed to address Saddam's concerns.

We had flown to Canada via Frankfurt and arrived in Toronto on July 17. Sons David and John met us at the airport. David took us to his apartment, then went back to work for a few hours. In the evening we went to Brown's Bistro for dinner.

Next day Allan and I went our separate ways. I had a hair appointment with Etheline, which Gillian (whom we often call Jill) had arranged, and Allan popped into Harry Rosen's on Bloor near Bay to buy a suit. Later he flew to Ottawa for meetings with External Affairs officials and others from Protocol and the Prime Minister's Office to plan for Prince Salman's September visit, with his 60-member entourage, to open "The Kingdom Yesterday and Today" exhibit. Allan had dinner with our son Chris, and admired his new white car.

Allan returned to Toronto on Friday. We were lucky to have the use of David's car throughout our stay. We drove to Port Colborne to spend the weekend with Nana and Grandpa.

Next day was sunny and beautiful for the shower that Allan's sister, Anne, gave for Siobhan. We had a delightful lunch in the garden behind the Gebhart house in Queenston.

David and Siobhan married in Holy Rosary Church on St Clair Avenue, and a charming reception followed at the Sutton Place Hotel. Beautiful music, delicious hors d'oeuvres, and delightful friends and relatives accompanied the speeches made in their honour.

But I rush to tell what happened August 3! Allan and I had just finished provisioning our boat, which was tied up in Pickering, on the lake east of Toronto, for a two-week sail. The refrigerator groaned with eggs, juices and milk, piles of steak, chicken, and wieners for the barbecue, and, perhaps most important, bottles of tonic for the drinks to end each day on Lake Ontario. Gillian and her youngsters had just arrived so we could sail on our eagerly anticipated journey to the Thousand Islands at the lake's far eastern end.

Then bulletins shouted and headlines erupted. Overnight Iraq had invaded and, indeed, conquered its small neighbour – Kuwait.

I watched Allan rush over to the public telephone at the end of the dock. As Canada's ambassador to Saudi Arabia, he knew it was urgent to call Ottawa to find out what had happened. Listening intently, he heard this dreadful piece of news that had shocked and surprised the entire international community. The attack came as a surprise to everyone. Iraq had been threatening to take over some disputed territory with oil wells, but neither experts nor any diplomats had expected this full-scale invasion. Not only were we enjoying our summer holiday, but also U.S. Ambassador Bodine in Kuwait was travelling in Europe blissfully unaware of trouble to come. Indeed, Larry Dickenson, Canada's new ambassador to Bahrain, Kuwait, Oman, Qatar, and the United Arab Emirates (UAE) — all former British protectorates on the eastern, Gulf side of the Arabian peninsula — had left Kuwait only 15 minutes before the invasion. Landing in Vienna, he tried to return — impossible.

In the early hours of the morning Iraq had invaded Kuwait. With a million 'battle-hardened' soldiers, compared with a few thousand in the Kuwaiti armed forces, Iraq had easily conquered its tiny neighbour. The emir of Kuwait escaped to Saudi Arabia, but his brother was killed trying to defend the palace. This family had ruled Kuwait for 254 years.

Then and there, Allan and I changed our plans. We were on our sailboat when all this began. Our small grandson, Patrick, had been with us at Hanlan's Point on Toronto Island, and we returned to Pickering, still having a lovely visit with him, joined by the rest of the family.

Allan contacted both Ottawa and Riyadh as soon as he heard the news. At that point they felt there was no need for him to return. However, by Saturday morning it was clear that he should be in Riyadh, able to help. Commercial counsellor Ron Bollman was chargé, and he and first secretary David Hutchings were carrying a very heavy load without time even to sleep.

We unloaded all those delectable provisions. Jill and her youngsters paraded silently down the dock to their car, carrying their loads of fine food to enjoy in their back yard or put in their basement freezer. Allan and I left the boat early Sunday morning, drove to Port Colborne quickly to see Nana and Grandpa, dashed to the airport, and flew out of Toronto at 3 p.m.

On August 6, when we reached the official Canadian residence in the Diplomatic Quarter in Riyadh, our long-serving, loyal household staff greeted us — the head man, Ali, first, followed by Hanif, the cook, and Zafar.

And again I focused on provisions, this time an abundance of food, for Canadians evacuating from the Eastern Province, which was oh-so-close to the border with Kuwait. Would Saddam's forces, having seized Kuwait, continue on into the Saudi oilfields? Would all those oil workers from Calgary and other parts of Alberta working for Aramco (Arabian American Oil Company, now Saudi Arabian Oil Company) have to flee? Indeed, would those of us living in Riyadh need to take to the desert, moving west towards Jeddah, to escape the fearsome Iraqi Republican Guards?

So my first thoughts turned towards sustenance.

"Ali, where can we start?" I bought for the freezer 20 chickens, three roasts of lamb, and many pounds of hamburger. Ali bought 300 riyals worth of fresh vegetables. Cases of water, lots of bread. With the large residence and the possibility of many guests, I had to prepare.

It was difficult for me to sleep. Journalists had been calling from Canada for interviews during the night. Once awake, I found it hard to go back to sleep. My stomach was churning! It reminded me of the feeling I had when we were caught sailing in a line squall on Lake Erie. I'm reluctant to label it 'fear,' but I guess I ain't no hero.

Thursday, August 9, 1990

I HEARD ON BBC RADIO a few minutes ago that Yemen had agreed to allow Iraq to use its airfields. Apparently Saddam Hussein has promised someday to return the Assir (the fertile area around Abha in southwestern Saudi Arabia) to the Yemenis, who believe the territory rightfully belongs to them. During the Iran--Iraq War, Yemen had sided with Iraq, and it was determined to do that again. Oh dear.

Last night around 10 p.m. the first Canadian family from Dammam (capital of the Eastern Province, on the Persian Gulf) arrived on our doorstep. They were travelling with an American and a British family and were checking in. The British have been making arrangements to house people in their school and at British Aerospace if necessary. I don't know what the Americans are planning. We continue to suggest to people in the Eastern Province that they may wish to consider having dependants and non-essential workers leave the area. So far there is not the same urgency for people in other areas of the Kingdom to leave.

Passports pose a problem.

"Employers hold the passports and arrange for exit visas. In King Fahad National Guard Hospital, the passport office is closed for the weekend," Allan sputtered in frustration.

Thus nurses who are anxious to leave are unable to get their documentation, even though they have been successful in reserving seats on planes. The embassy will issue another passport to them in an emergency. In fact that was done yesterday, but the man who went to the airport with the new passport was turned back because he had neither his entry visa (which would be in the passport held by the employer) nor an exit visa, which the Ministry of Foreign Affairs issues to the employer.

There are about five thousand Canadians in Saudi Arabia — mostly doctors and nurses in Jeddah and Riyadh, and oilmen and their families in Dhahran. Dhahran and Al Khobar form a 'triple city' with Dammam. The Saudi Ministry of Foreign Affairs has told Allan that its officials would issue exit visas at the airport in Dammam, but so far they are not doing that in Riyadh. We are maintaining contact daily with the Canadians in each area — Dammam, Jeddah, and Riyadh. Those like me who are answering calls are checking to be sure the callers' names and telephone numbers are on our lists. I feel so sorry for nurses whose families are urging them to leave, but who feel a responsibility to stay to help if there are to be war injuries.

CHAPTER 8

CALLING ALL CANADIANS

Wednesday, August 15, 1990

IT HAS BEEN A BUSY WEEK. My job at the embassy has been to use the computer in Donald McLennan's office — he's our minister-counsellor (commercial) — to input data on all the Canadians in the Jeddah area, including Yanbu and Abha, and also the information we have been receiving from the United Arab Emirates since the embassy staff in Kuwait can no longer look after the other Gulf states.

The system in place provided a foundation with which to begin. Many Canadians had already registered with the embassy even though they are not required to. (In fact, some people had not done so, fearing that somehow the information would be passed on to Revenue Canada and would affect them adversely. They need not hesitate for that reason, because there is no such connection. The reason for registering is now becoming evident to everyone! We need to know who and where they are so we can contact them in an emergency. Now there are many phone calls from Canadians who want us to know they are here.)

Ottawa had taken the responsibility for entering information into computer form; as soon as this emergency arose they sent the computerized list to us. But their list didn't include phone numbers! Andrew Shisko quickly devised a very simple format for us to get necessary information together using both the Ottawa lists and the registration forms in our files. We used the following categories: name, number in family, place, company, home phone, office phone, and status (are they here or have they left). Andrew worked on the Eastern Province while I helped him by doing the UAE, including Abu Dhabi, Dubai, etc. I did the Jeddah file, and several others worked on Riyadh.

We contacted key people in each of the areas — those we knew could be counted on to swing into action to communicate with their fellow Canadians in an emergency. Some 20 people in Riyadh, 15 in Jeddah, and another dozen or more in the Eastern Province agreed to act as 'wardens,' who would pass along information as needed.

Once we had quick and dirty lists, we sent them by fax to the wardens in each of the areas. They were expected to let us know of additions, corrections, and deletions. (Many of the people on our lists might have gone: some having left at the end of their contract without letting us know; others having left recently because of the current crisis.)

A written notice was sent to all the wardens for distribution. It said that Canadian dependants and non-essential employees in the Eastern Province might wish to consider leaving. It urged people to ensure they were registered, and it told them about the warden system of contacting those who were on our lists.

Thursday, August 16, 1990

WE HAD BEEN BACK IN RIYADH ONLY TEN DAYS. American troops had already started arriving in Saudi Arabia. We listened hourly to the BBC short-wave radio to hear of developments. Apparently there were about 50 warships in the Persian Gulf. We heard through the news that 4,000 American troops were on the way. We saw confidential reports that as many as 200,000 were being mobilized. I had opposed the U.S.-led invasion of Grenada (1983) and its invasion of Panama (1989), and my relief at American involvement here surprised me.

Condemnation by other countries was almost unanimous. The United Nations applied sanctions against Iraqi trade and was debating a resolution to condemn the annexation of Kuwait. Britain sent ships and planes to support Saudi Arabia. President Hosni Mubarak of Egypt called an emergency Arab summit. "This is the last chance for Iraq to withdraw from Kuwait or face destructive consequences."

At the moment of the invasion, Larry Dickenson, Canada's new envoy to Kuwait and the smaller Gulf states, had landed in Vienna on his vacation, only to find out that he must try to return to Kuwait immediately. He had been trying unsuccessfully ever since. Airports have closed in Kuwait, so he flew to Saudi Arabia. He stayed in our residence Friday night and made contact through telex with his chargé d'affaires, Bill Bowden, in the Canadian embassy's communications room in Kuwait. He left Saturday afternoon in one of our cars, accompanied by second secretaries Albert Galpin (political) and Andrew Shisko (commercial) and in convoy with a group of British diplomats making their way to the border to try to help their nationals escape across. Larry tried four times to cross the border but was turned back by

Iraqi military each time. He finally drove back here yesterday and is spending his time in efforts to contact Canadians in Bahrain to advise evacuation. In the meantime all communication links with the Canadian embassy in Kuwait have been severed. Allan went with Larry to the airport around 6 in the morning. Ottawa was sending Larry to Amman, Jordan, where he would link up with David Karsgard, who had just finished as our ambassador to Iraq. They were both to go to Baghdad. Then Larry would try to go on to Kuwait from there. There still was no direct communication with our embassy in Kuwait, but the Danes, who had radio equipment, were passing messages to our people there. (Allan was trying to get Ottawa to provide the same sort of radio equipment here before we lost our links with the outside world.) I think Larry was pretty apprehensive about his mission.

My diary went on:

ALLAN MEETS REGULARLY WITH THE AMBASSADORS of New Zealand and Australia. They have established a working group to share evacuation plans. Ron Bollman is our designated member of their small committee. He is addressing such specifics as where one of our Hercules planes might land if the airports are closed at a time when we must be evacuating Canadians (on a highway or also on the gravelly desert). He also had a briefing at the American embassy this week.

Embassy staffers have set up the multi-purpose room to receive evacuees from Kuwait if necessary. Ottawa has sent a technician with up-to-date radio equipment to be installed on the roof for communication if conventional telephone and telex lines are cut. We have walkie-talkie type equipment in our study and bedroom and in each of the staff houses in the Diplomatic Quarter as well as in the embassy.

Six Canadian soldiers are expected to arrive here at the embassy next week. They will guard our establishment, and will also be useful if it turns out that our evacuation plans have to be put into effect. Allan is suggesting to people in the Eastern Province that they may wish to consider having dependants and non-essential workers leave the area. Still, the passport problem persists. Employers hold the passports, and arrange for exit visas. In his addresses to Canadians in all parts of the country, Allan explains that the embassy will issue another passport to them in emergency situations.

We are keeping contact daily with the Canadians in each area. Andrew Shisko talks to those in the Eastern Province, and also in Bahrain and the United Arab Emirates; Albert Galpin contacts Canadians in Riyadh; and Ron Bollman is calling Canadians in Jeddah, Abha, etc. Those like me who are answering calls are checking to be sure the callers' names and telephone numbers are on our lists. Allan has full staff meetings in the morning and evening to be sure everyone is fully informed. The group are working really well together.

The Australian embassy is evacuating all its dependants. So far it is the only coalition partner we know of that is doing that now.

The press has been trying very hard to get into Saudi Arabia, and Allan has been trying to help. He has been in touch with the deputy minister of information, who as recently as yesterday said he would seek authorization from the minister. Allan gives all live interviews to radio and television. Ron Bollman handles the rest of the press. Unfortunately, however, many newsmen have our residence phone number (it is printed in the official book of Canadian Representatives Abroad). Almost every night the phone has rung with journalists pursuing their questions in the middle of the night. It's pretty tough when the day has been so intense to have one's sleep interrupted like that. However, Allan is wonderfully patient.

Allan is going to King Fahad National Guard Hospital to speak to Canadians about the crisis. If that meeting seems to be useful, he can do the same thing at King Faisal Hospital.

Tuesday, August 21, 1990

IT IS 6:45 P.M. AND ALLAN IS IN THE MIDST of a meeting with Canadians in Dammam. He flew out early this morning with Andrew Shisko, and should return by midnight tonight. He feels an obligation to go to the Eastern Province to let our people know that someone cares. He'll reiterate the Canadian government's advice that consideration should be given to departure of non-essential workers and all dependants. He will also tell them that he has an evacuation plan in place, without going into a lot of detail. (For example, the advice that will be given if bombs should fall in the Eastern Province is that people should move towards Riyadh.) The embassy staff has been developing evacuation contingencies such as the logistics of arranging buses, planes, and so on, as a response to different events. All very complicated.

Before meeting the Canadians today, Allan had a meeting with the deputy governor of the Eastern Province and also with the vice-president of Aramco, who is in charge of personnel. In this way he hopes to have additional up-to-date information to pass along to the Canadians.

He expects to return to Riyadh on a plane at either 9 or 10 o'clock. One holds one's breath while waiting for him to return from such a potentially dangerous area. I thought how interesting it would be to hear if he has seen any evidence of the military buildup in the region or has spotted all the ships in the Gulf as his plane lands.

Newspapers and BBC short-wave radio tell us today that President Bush is being very firm about his objectives of having Iraq retire from Kuwait and allow the former regime to be re-established. He seems to have UN support for his desire to take military action to enforce the blockade of trade with Iraq.

At the same time, Saddam Hussein has publicly announced that foreigners are being relocated as shields to strategic military and civilian installations to prevent attack upon the installations. He seems already to be moving U.S. and French nationals as well as British citizens and threatens to do the same with people from any country that is sending forces in opposition to him. As far as I know, it is not clear yet what will happen to Canadians. The advice given by Ottawa has been for them to stay hidden in their homes but not to resist if forced.

Saddam Hussein has also announced that all embassy personnel must leave Kuwait by Friday, August 24, because Kuwait is now only a 'province' of Iraq. Any embassy people staying behind would no longer have their diplomatic immunity and would be subject to the same treatment as any other foreigners. So far, the U.S., Britain, and Canada are determined to keep their embassies operating. You have to feel awfully sorry for the people who are stuck there. It must be terribly frightening.

Jean-François, a young Canadian diplomat from Kuwait who was on holidays with his family and had expected to return only a day or so after the invasion, is enormously relieved that his family is able to stay in Canada; meanwhile, he has come here to take up duties in the consular section because we now have to handle all the Kuwait stuff.

I have worked long hours for the past couple of days, updating the database of Canadians in the western part of the Kingdom, including Jeddah, Abha, and Yanbu. Maiz Teriaky is our man in Jeddah. He has recruited 14 'wardens' or telephone volunteers and divided up the list amongst them. The volunteers have contacted all the people and have passed along to me any revisions to our file. It has been a lot of work, but we're in good shape now. And, quite frankly, I've enjoyed working on it. In the long run, Albert (who is responsible for the consular section) will be really happy to have such a valuable list. (The Australians have just begun to create such a list and are fumbling around trying to use Word Perfect. They asked Colin Suter, Pam Saunders's husband, who works independently in the Kingdom, if he would set them up in Dbase. As a matter of fact the Irish embassy has also asked Colin to get a system going for them too.)

I don't think that it is a case of us all being behind the times regarding computers, but rather that this seemed such a stable environment that no one attached great priority to having complete consular lists. We were all focusing on trade, I imagine. I recall hearing that a lot of Canadians had not registered with the embassy in spite of being notified that it was a good idea.

Allan did go to meet a few hundred people at King Faisal Hospital. A lot of interest was expressed in how people could send their possessions to Canada as a precaution without making the final decision to leave the Kingdom personally. In other words they are pretty interested in questions of Customs and income tax, Persian rugs, and cats, as well as evacuation plans, in case of war.

Allan was successful in persuading the Saudi government to allow journalists into the Kingdom. They agreed to receive 12. Allan (very wisely) contacted Ottawa and asked them to negotiate with the press to determine who the people should be. They came back with a list of 13 and Allan feels that the Saudis will be cooperative about that number. He hopes they will arrive in Riyadh so that he can brief them over lunch here at the residence.

One of the embassy staff, Ron Bollman, told me this morning that he was expecting to see a journalist from the *Los Angeles Times*. Apparently the Americans who were allowed in a few days ago are finding it difficult to get people to talk. People he are not used to a free press and no doubt not willing to be quoted in case they get into trouble. Actually, Ron was going to use his chat with the reporter to find out how the Saudis are treating the press and what ground rules they are imposing. It will be useful in helping our guys.

Allan has been instructed to call on the emir of Kuwait who has taken refuge in Saudi Arabia. There is a letter from our prime minister [Brian Mulroney] to deliver. The Kuwaiti ambassador to Saudi Arabia came to Allan's office yesterday. He will let Allan know when his appointment with the emir will be — likely Tuesday or Wednesday in Taif. Allan and David Hutchings will fly to Jeddah. Atta will drive ahead so he can drive them to Taif. While in Jeddah, they may have an opportunity to meet with Canadians to give them the same sort of briefing he gave those in Dammam and Riyadh. I hope they won't try to crowd too many functions into one day. Allan is willing to be away from the embassy only one night because of responsibilities here. His trip to Dammam was pretty strenuous.

Monday, August 27, 1990

SO ALLAN IS INDEED OFF TO SEE THE EMIR. Atta drove ahead very early today to be in Jeddah to meet him at the airport if possible. They will drive to Taif tomorrow morning for a 1 p.m. meeting with the emir, then back to Jeddah to meet the 14 wardens who are responsible for contacting about 800 Canadians in the Western Province. Before he left, Allan signed letters addressed to the wardens of the Eastern Province. They continue to give the same advice, but add that the Canadian military presence at the embassy is helpful in finalizing evacuation plans. He attached a list of things like water, fuel, and clothes to have in their cars ready for evacuation if necessary. (Reminds me of a clothing list for Camp Kandalore in the Algonquin Highlands, where our grandchildren spent many summers.) He also asked the wardens to identify points in their districts, which could serve as meeting places if a convoy were to be formed. He intends to send another letter to all the people still in Dammam when he returns from Jeddah. The people at the embassy are working on completing mail addresses in our computer files. (Up till now, we have considered it most important to have telephone numbers. The addresses will be useful now that there is time.)

How vicariously I live! All these details are about Allan. And yet surely that's what history is about, and I feel as if this diary is perhaps a worthwhile chronicle of what is happening in one tiny segment of the Middle East during a crisis of major proportions. And Canada is already in up to its eyebrows, with preparations under way for Operation Friction, and we in the Riyadh embassy will be very close to the action.

Sunday, September 16, 1990

ALLAN HAS GONE TO YEMEN to meet Foreign Minister Abd Al-Karim Al-Iryani. Meanwhile, I received a call from Donald McLennan, who is chargé d'affaires while Allan is out of the country, telling me that the Iraqis have opened the border between Kuwait and

Saudi Arabia. Many Kuwaitis who have had their passports and other identification taken from them have crossed the border. So far there is no word whether third-country nationals are being allowed out. There are about 60 Canadians still in Kuwait, and this may provide their opportunity to leave. Albert Galpin has left in a car with one of our Canadian soldiers to go to the border town of Al Khafgi to help any Canadians. A British consul is going along with him in a second car. (Speculation about the removal of passports is as follows: a) They want to empty all the Kuwaitis out of Kuwait so that Iraqis can move in and take over permanently; and b) They will use the passports for terrorists.)

According to Donald, there are a lot of calls from the press about this latest development. Ron Bollman is handling the inquiries, so I'll be able to give reporters his home phone number when they call during the night.

Allan's meeting in Yemen was interesting. He spent an hour and twenty minutes with the foreign minister, so has lots to report to Ottawa. The Scandinavian ambassadors, along with those from New Zealand and Australia, are asking him for a briefing.

He found an enormous amount of anti-Western sentiment in Sana'a. During the long Iran-Iraq War, Yemen had sent thousands of its men to support Iraq.

During a breakfast meeting with the American ambassador and another with the British ambassador there, both told him about demonstrations that have taken place as protests against the Saudis as well as the West. Their countries have issued advice for their citizens to leave. We have 27 Canadians in Sana'a. Allan will send to them similar advice.

Last night at a casual dinner party at the new official residence of Turkey I sat next to Alaudeen Alaskary, who is head of communications in the Ministry of Foreign Affairs (MFA) here. He told us how very worried the Saudis are about possible agitation among the Yemenis living here. Alex McGoldrick (Australian ambassador) was also at my table. Apparently the Saudi authorities had arrested his Yemeni driver about six weeks earlier. Alaudeen said the matter had been discussed at the daily management meeting at the MFA; he was trying to persuade Alex to try to understand their concern and their need to 'investigate' the driver's activities. He asked Alex to back off, but Alex is quite incensed and would have none of it.

And it was interesting to read the press next morning about the decision to revoke privileges formally held by Yemenis resident in Saudi Arabia. Previously they had been the only foreigners allowed to work here without a sponsor. They had been able to secure a visa at the airport, and had been allowed to invest and own businesses. All that has been stopped.

A Canadian general and other high-level military types have just flown to Bahrain with Larry Dickenson in a Canadian Challenger in order to arrange to 'park' our 18 aircraft there. To their surprise, I guess, they found that there is no room. (Sounds like the Mad Hatter's tea party — might they not have checked that out before?) Apparently they have discovered, too, that the central organizing is taking place in Riyadh. There was an urgent call last evening asking Allan to arrange for them to come to Riyadh to consult Americans and Saudis. They have no visas, etc., but David Hutchings got going right away (in our study) to see if arrangements could be made.

Then a couple of hours later Allan received word that Ottawa wanted our guys in Bahrain to 'stand down' (that now-infamous term) for 24 hours so that our military in Ottawa could consult with the Pentagon and State Department. These are the types who are going to protect us all. Hope they figure it out soon.

Bab al-Yaman, Yemen Gate, and below, street scene;
both in the old city, Sana'a

Concert *in the* Sky

Friday, September 21, 1990

NICK AND ANNA COCKING SUGGESTED we go with them to a concert on the desert that the expat community was putting on. We had wanted to do that ever since we heard about the monthly event. So, Cockings went home to pack a lunch and returned in their Range Rover for us at 5:30 p.m.

We drove out over the escarpment on the highway, then turned off onto a rocky, winding sand and gravel track through the desert. It's amazing what a four-wheel drive recreation vehicle can do on the desert terrain, and one can understand the necessity for them.

The venue for the concert is in the middle of a crater-like formation of rocks. People bring picnics, and settle into comfortable niches in the rocky hill with mattresses and, in our case, folding chairs. It was dark when the concert began at 7 p.m. Lights were turned off, and only half a dozen pinpoints of light of flashlights could be seen on the hills, which formed a circle like a natural amphitheatre.

The music was very pleasant — a program that Nick correctly likened to Boston Pops. Much of it was made up of excerpts from best-loved favourites of opera: *The Marriage of Figaro, La Gioconda, The Barber of Seville, Cavalleria Rusticana, Madame Butterfly, Tristan und Isolde,* and *Die Meistersinger.* It was a concert actually from compact disc (seemed funny to clap at the end of a piece, but you felt like registering appreciation somehow), and the speaker system was well placed to give an excellent quality of sound.

Sitting on the edges of the hills surrounding this 'crater' in the dark under a clear sky filled with stars hanging close over our heads created the impression of belonging to a group of the only humans on the planet, clinging to the last vestiges of civilization as we listened to such fine classical music. (No doubt the potential of war has its effect on the imagination.)

Another image was that of belonging to some group of humans on another planet somewhere in outer space. (I've seen too many movies.) I was reminded, too, of a classic American play, Thornton Wilder's *Our Town*, where the ghosts of previous inhabitants of a small town sat in chairs in the 'cemetery' at the edge of the stage and commented on the actions of the players. We too sat like shadows on the hills surrounding pure sound. The next concert will be October 4 under a full moon. I'll be in Greece with my sister, Ruth, by that time, bringing her back to Riyadh to complete her adventure.

Highway to the desert

Saturday, September 29, 1990

ALLAN SPENT THURSDAY with Brigadier-General Jean Boyle, commander of the Canadian forces in Germany, who had come to negotiate a home base for our planes. It seemed that the British had found Doha, in Qatar, on the Persian Gulf, too expensive to supply so had moved away, leaving space there.

Thursday evening, Allan entertained Major-General Eric Olson (no. 2 in the U.S. military in Saudi Arabia) and a colonel, along with General Boyle, and our guys Ron Bollman, David Hutchings, and Donald McLennan. Because I had another dinner to attend, I met them only briefly but found them charming. It is interesting that men who have risen to the top of a tightly disciplined organization — who give orders and expect exact regimentation of troops, with all the spit and polish that entails — can appear to be so relaxed, cordial, and pleasant.

My dinner party was at the residence of the ambassador of Nigeria, hosted by both his wives! It was a farewell party for the wife of the ambassador from Gambia. Most of the guests were from the African countries, and most spoke French and Arabic. The women's national dresses are gorgeous! They sported full gowns in wonderful patterns of pink, green, blue. Their various shapes of turbans and headdresses complete some great outfits. Dinner was a buffet served outside, after the usual preliminary sitting in huge, comfortable chairs in the living-room. After dinner the ladies danced in a large circle, gently moving from side to side. I was sorry to have to leave at that point, because Atta had to return to take General Boyle to the airport for a flight back to Germany.

The following evening we had about 60 Canadians for a reception to thank the wardens in the Riyadh area for helping keep their compatriots informed during the ongoing crisis.

In Sana'a, Italy and other nations have helped restore lovely old
mud buildings, several stories high, all joined together.
Yemenis customarily decorate their windows with a sort of whitewash
known as alabaster to indicate they have taken part in the hajj.

Mykonos, Greece

CHAPTER 9

CHANGE *of* PACE

Greece (October 1990)

MY SISTER, RUTH HUTCHINSON, and I had planned a great trip to Greece. She had intended to come on to Saudi Arabia with me at the end of our vacation, but had cancelled her air ticket because of the ongoing hostilities.

I flew to Athens to meet her on Tuesday, October 2. She had already spent about three days in Crete. She had returned to Athens by overnight ferry and had arrived at our hotel about 8 o'clock in the morning. Fortunately, the hotel was able to give her a room, because she had an intestinal upset by that time. When I arrived around 5 p.m., Ruth was in bed. She roused herself, however, and we started a really good visit.

Our first four days were taken up with a guided tour of the Peloponnese. This turned out to be very interesting and informative. We visited Corinth, where the canal allows shipping to pass from the Aegean to the Ionian Sea. Then we went on to Napflion, which is a delightful village on the water, surrounded by beautiful hills. Ruth and I spent some time walking about the village while the tour went on to Epidaurus. We enjoyed taking pictures from the hills looking down on attractive, orange-tiled roofs.

Our tour took us to the ruins of Mycenae and the famous tomb of Agamemnon. Subsequent days included the ancient site of Olympia and, finally, Delphi, which is situated high in a mountain with spectacular views.

"I can't resist taking pictures of these cypress trees on the mountainside. They're beautiful!" Thank goodness we had bought a camera in Athens. It would have seemed unforgivably remiss not to have equipment to record such an interesting trip.

There were some pleasant people on the tour. A group of four women from Vancouver had already been touring Turkey for about 12 days, and were finding it a bit strenuous. There were also two American couples with whom we chatted frequently, and a cute young couple from Paris — she works in the 'Bourse' (stock exchange), and he works in their Ministry of Finance.

The tour bus dropped us off at our hotel in Athens around 6 p.m. on Saturday, and, rather than spending a night in Athens, which is not terrifically attractive, we decided to fly right away to the island of Mykonos. There we were met by the owner of a little pension (Stellio). He drove us into town and led us up stairways and alleys to our room. It was tiny, attractive, clean, and cheap. (In fact we paid no more than $30 per night throughout our trip in the islands. Divided by two, those are pretty satisfactory rates!)

Ruth carried Frommer's guidebook *Greece on $35 a Day*. It was really invaluable. It was much more readable than my Baedeker, and had helpful suggestions about places to visit, restaurants with reasonable prices, and inexpensive hotels. It was a bit of a game for Ruth, and I had decided I would go along with all of it.

(I must admit the toughest part was carrying luggage from ferries to hotels and vice-versa because Ruth refused to take a taxi.) We took buses when possible, and trudged from place to place. It was particularly satisfying to return to Riyadh and find that I had a whole lot of money left!

Mykonos is very attractive, and we had a lovely view from our tiny balcony over the harbourfront. The town reminded me a bit of Provincetown at the end of Cape Cod. It was very quaint in a sort of artificial way. I had the impression that Mykonos was a very popular place for tourists because it had made itself picturesque for that purpose. Anyway, Ruth agreed with my suggestion that we move on next day to a more rugged island that the books said is inhabited more by Greeks than by tourists.

Before leaving Mykonos, we took a short ferry-ride to the island of Delos. The young French couple on our guided tour had told us we must be sure to see the archaeological digs there. It really was interesting, particularly in light of what we had learned about ancient Greek history on our trip.

Our next move was to the island of Tinos, a couple of hours by ferry from Mykonos. The ferries are much like the ones we took to cross the Channel between Dover and Calais. Our hotel there was fine — larger room with very high ceiling and a balcony overlooking the harbour. (Showers were almost invariably without curtains in our accommodations on the islands. It is quite a challenge to use the hand-held sprayer and try not to have a flood of water all over the bathroom.) We decided to settle in for two nights. It was a pleasure to unpack and feel at home.

Weather was beautiful the entire time we were in Greece. Hot and sunny, with blue skies just like Riyadh. October is the end of the tourist season, but it was perfect for us. I had bought a new windbreaker, thinking that it might be chilly on the sea, but I used it only once, on the way back to Athens.

We wandered around Tinos, up the narrow street with shops to a lovely old monastery, and along the seashore in search of the dozens of dovecotes for which the island is famous. (In our search for dovecotes we were somewhat hindered by the fact that we didn't know what they looked like! At first we thought the bell-towers of churches were homes of the doves. Later we realized they were separate square structures located all over the island.) We also took a local bus to the end of the island. There we had a lunch of fresh fish at a little restaurant, then walked a half-mile or so to a beautiful sandy beach, which we had all to ourselves for swimming.

Our final island was Andros. We agreed to splurge on a B-class hotel that was located outside of the town where our ferry left us. Our room was on a hill looking out on a lovely beach and blue-green water of the Aegean. As soon as we unpacked, we set off on a hike of several miles to the village of Betzi. I have lots of pictures of it because it really was a pretty walk. There, Ruth bought snorkel and mask so that we could both go snorkelling in a lovely bay on our way back to the hotel. (I had never done that, and found it added a whole new dimension to swimming. I'd really like to go snorkelling in the Red Sea.)

Ruth had left her decision as to whether she would come on to Riyadh until near the end of our holiday in Greece. She had determined that unless a shot had been fired she would come. So back to Riyadh we both came, arriving about 1:30 a.m. Allan and Atta met us at the airport, and at last we were able to have some help with the bags!

Ruth *in* Riyadh

R UTH ENJOYED HER STAY in the Saudi capital. We did lots of sight-seeing: went to the top of the TV Tower and had a tour of the television studios in the Ministry of Information; explored the Museum of Archaeology; were guided through the unfinished building of the Ministry of the Interior with its spaceship; and paid a couple of visits to the Dira souk in the heart of the city. We also had lots of social engagements. The Gaarders (Norway) were leaving; hence a merry round of farewell luncheons, teas, receptions, and dinners. Ruth began to feel like old buddies with some of the women. We also had a couple of lunches in Saudi homes. That provided an interesting experience too. She was here only a week, but we packed a lot in.

We visited Al Diriyah, northwest of Riyadh, the first capital of the House of Saud. The Ottoman Empire had destroyed the city

Nora as a Saudi guest

Typical crenellation of Saudi architecture:
Left: Masmak Fort (clay and mud brick), historic centre, Riyadh
Bottom: Saad bin Saud Palace, Al Diriyah

Traditional doorways, Saad bin Saud Palace: a substantially restored highlight of Al Diriyah's at-Tarif district, which is a UNESCO World Heritage Site

early in the 19th century, Ruth noted, but it was restored in the 1970s. It was the seedbed of Wahhabi Muslim fundamentalism.

As we explored the ruins of Al Diriyah, we encountered an elderly, bearded man in turban and long, soiled garments. In the Saudi tradition, he invited us to follow along to what seemed like a dugout in rock where he served us coffee.

When she returned to Michigan, Ruth wrote about her Saudi experience in the *Grand Rapids Press*. She worried about the pending war: "The architecture of Riyadh, capital of Saudi Arabia, is a potential casualty of the Gulf War ... The Saudis have built, or have under construction, striking palaces, conference centers, ministries, embassies and shopping malls. Walls of gleaming glass reflect adobe buildings."

Ruth described the most unusual building in the Diplomatic Quarter — the Tuwaiq Palace. An international competition in 1981 awarded Omrania & Associates of Riyadh, in association with Frei Otto and Buro Happold, design and site supervision of what was to be called the Diplomatic Club. Basem al Shihabi, a good friend of Allan's, was principal architect.

Ruth described Tuwaiq's circular wall the colour of traditional adobe. Inside she had seen buildings with white fibreglass roofs shaped like tents, bowling alleys, squash courts, swimming pools, and an auditorium for 300! This was to be a conference centre but, to my knowledge, has not by any means yet met its potential.

Steve Martin Drops In

ONE OF OUR 'EVENTS' DURING RUTH'S VISIT was a dinner party for 40 in our garden. We experimented with the elegant touch that David and Siobhan had had at their wedding reception

— music. We had a violin and cello in the front hall as guests arrived, then in the garden during dinner. It may have been a bit too loud indoors with the crowd of people, but it was lovely outside.

We had some unexpected guests accompanying the Freemans (U.S.). They brought Steve Martin and his wife, Victoria Tennant! What fun! One had to giggle just in saying 'hello' to him. He sat at my table and seemed like a very sensitive, nice person. Most of our guests knew him; some British types like the Cockings knew her better because she is a British actress. Others such as the Van Eses and Saudis didn't know them at all.

The Martins had just arrived during the previous night, so had had time only for a briefing by U.S. General Norman Schwarzkopf, who was heading Operation Desert Shield (Canada's Operation Friction coordinates very closely with it). The next day they were going to visit troops, but not to perform (the Americans are being really discreet in the Saudi cultural environment), only meet people and talk to them personally.

Pat Freeman wrote in her thank-you note that Steve Martin had been a bit apprehensive about meeting Saudis at our house. He worried that he didn't know enough about their customs and might commit some gaffe. As it turned out, she said, he enjoyed his conversations with them.

During the course of dinner I mentioned to him that I had felt a bit hesitant about issuing invitations a couple of weeks earlier because we didn't know what the status of the crisis would be, and it would be a pity to be engaging in revelry on the eve of war. He said the same sort of thought had crossed his mind, reminding him of scenes from E.M. Forster's *A Passage to India*. (I recall bits of a poem by Lord Byron we studied in school when I was a child. It was about the dining and dancing on "The Eve of Waterloo": "There was a sound of revelry by night ... ")

In the residence garden and on the patio,
Madiha Al Agaroush created a souk as it might appear
in Abha, October 1990.

CHAPTER 10

BUILDING BRIDGES

Friday, October 19, 1990

THIS WEEK WAS BUSY with women's coffee parties. The Canadians of Riyadh held a morning coffee here and invited the American association as guests. So we had about 120 people. Dr Madiha Al Agaroush (a very up-and-coming young Saudi woman writer and photographer) made a presentation about the book about Abha and the surrounding area that she and two other Saudi women had produced against all odds. They self-published *Abha, Bilad Asir: South-Western Region of the Kingdom of Saudi Arabia* (Riyadh 1989), which is a handsome volume. Madiha decorated our residence garden and patio to look like the Tuesday souk at Abha, complete with handmade baskets and carpets and jugs and bowls. It really was very attractive and interesting. I think the women enjoyed it very much indeed.

I had promised Madiha that I would invite my diplomatic friends for a second morning in order to make all her effort worthwhile. So Allan's assistant had sent invitations to a bunch

An arabesque of ambassadors' wives

of ambassadors' wives and some others I had on my list, and we had a very nice party the next day with them. Hanif made apricot bread, carrot cake, date-nut loaf, lemon bread, and numerous pastries, as well as trays of sandwiches, etc. Allan is using the leftovers to have a little embassy get-together at 3:30 this afternoon to introduce some of the new staffers who have joined us recently.

The Canadian chief of defence staff, along with the deputy minister of defence, is to arrive here for a short visit next week. At this moment Allan and his gang are in a state of anxiety because the Saudis have not come up with their program of meetings yet. As always, the uncertainty and inability to tie details down are a killer. We have planned a super dinner for 22 men for the occasion. Hope all goes well.

Friday, October 26, 1990

ALLAN AND I HAVE JUST SWUM A HALF-MILE, and Allan has gone over to the embassy to check on developments.

We were at a delightful dinner party Wednesday night at the Plumblys. Derek is deputy head of mission for the British embassy. His wife, Nadia, is Egyptian by birth. They had a very pleasant group. I found particular satisfaction in being able to identify relationships between people I met that evening and people I already knew. For example, I had a good chat with Rema Shihabi, who sat at my table in the garden. I asked her if she were any relation to Nadia Shihabi. When she replied that Nadia was her sister-in-law, I was able to say, "Then you must be daughter-in-law of the Saudi ambassador to the United Nations!" Right on.

Then I also met an enjoyable young woman whose husband was in the Saudi army and was to leave for the border with Kuwait next morning. It turned out that her father is Ambassador Zuhair, who has just been posted to Canada. I knew then that she is sister to Nadia Zayid, Sheikh Talal's wife in Jeddah. Nadia and Talal had had a wonderful dinner for us when we first arrived last autumn. So it is fun to sort these people out after being here a year. At least some things are getting a little clearer!

We met, too, a very dynamic woman, Wafia Lacey — also Egyptian originally (now American) — who is married to the Middle East head of the American construction and engineering giant Bechtel Corporation. She knows several people here, even though she arrived only about three weeks ago, because she had gone to school with them at Victoria College in Alexandria. Teymour Alireza (head of the Reyazat Group) was educated there too. It was the most popular institution with Saudis until they started seeking U.S. higher education.

Allan is accompanying Chief of Defence Staff (CDS) General John de Chastelain, Deputy Minister of Defence Bob Fowler, and Commodore Kenneth J. Summers, head of the Canadian armed forces in the Gulf (Operation Friction) in their meetings to integrate Canadian efforts with coalition forces, led by the Americans' Operation Desert Shield. I haven't heard how their morning was, but they returned from Jeddah feeling pretty frustrated by Defence Minister Prince Sultan's rude treatment of them. Too bad. They were with him only a short time and returned here early, so Allan brought them over for beer and sandwiches and coffee in the garden. Then they were off to another meeting in the Command Centre. Hope that is going well. They are to meet Canadian soldiers in our embassy's multi-purpose room (dubbed the Wadi Club) at 8:30 this evening, then come over for the dinner in their honour at 9.

Michael Shenstone is here to show interest on the part of the Middle East Task Force in Ottawa. As former ambassador here, he was delighted to see how lovely the new residence is. He had heard so many complaints from a predecessor that he had wondered what kind of architectural disaster it might be.

Monday, October 29, 1990

WE LEAVE TOMORROW FOR JUBAIL, the new industrial city on the Persian Gulf, in the Eastern Province. Jubail is one of the world's great engineering and construction projects, which the Saudi government began to build in 1975, with Bechtel as the leading player. Atta (our driver) is leaving early to be in Dhahran when we arrive by plane. So Wayne House (commercial counsellor) and I are going out to the airport for the 9:30 a.m. flight. We'll meet Allan there because he will be seeing our military people off a little earlier.

Friday, November 2, 1990

WE ARRIVED IN JUBAIL IN TIME FOR LUNCH on Tuesday with the afternoon free. It was a good chance for Allan to recover from his busy time with the CDS in Riyadh. For dinner at the hotel, nine Canadians joined us. These were the people acting as wardens for the approximately 70 Canadians in the area: Normand Benoit and his wife, Malcolm Lamb, Mr McCracken, and a couple from North Battleford, Saskatchewan. (I told them about my mother's visits there about 1915.)

Benoit and his wife are both studying with the University of Waterloo by correspondence — he in chemistry, and she in psychology. This really whetted my appetite for study. They very kindly dropped off a university calendar at our hotel next morning. I see a couple of courses in logic — something I've wanted to do for a long time. Or perhaps I should consider teaching English as a foreign language. That might be useful in the long run.

Malcolm Lamb was talking about the 'Pacific Circle' (around the Pacific) package tours that Cathay Pacific offers. He, too, kindly dropped off the relevant material to us at the hotel — so we have something to start with in planning a holiday during Ramadan, the ninth month — for fasting — in the lunar Muslim calendar, March 18—April 15, 1991.

Next day we went to the spectacular headquarters for the Royal Commission of Jubail and Yanbu, which the government set up in 1975 to help orchestrate the diversification of the national economy and create industrial cities Jubail, on the Gulf, and Yanbu, on the Red Sea. Our friend Prince Abdullah bin Faisal bin Turki (Prince Abdullah) is chair of the Royal Commission. At its headquarters we saw an excellent presentation in the visitors' centre — a slide presentation followed by a tour of displays like the Ontario Science Centre in Toronto. Then a small bus took us to visit several plants. We now have been exposed to far more than we ever craved about the manufacture of steel, methanol propylene, ethylene, etc. The president of each company met us, served us coffee, and then guided us through the plant.

"How's your bladder holding up?" I whispered to Allan (as I felt concern about mine), but we held on till we were taken to lunch at about 3 p.m.

The Holiday Inn at Jubail is as nice as everyone had said, and we were in a very comfortable suite. We walked on the beach where mixed swimming is allowed. Later, Allan had a swim in the pool (no mixed swimming there!).

Thursday, we drove about two hours southeast to the island country of Bahrain. Wayne House was with us, and it was interesting for him to see that kingdom for the first time. The drive across the King Fahd Causeway connecting Saudi Arabia to the archipelago was lovely as always.

Larry Dickenson, our ambassador to Bahrain, Kuwait, Oman, Qatar, and the UAE, was setting up a small office in Bahrain's capital, Manama. He had us for drinks in his 'office' in the Intercontinental Hotel and then took us to the stunning Upstairs/Downstairs restaurant for dinner. Commodore Ken Summers came with us too from his local headquarters. He's a very nice, gentle person. Larry, as always, was full of entertaining gossip, so the evening was a pleasant one.

Our flight home from Dammam delivered us back to Riyadh by mid-afternoon, so Allan went over to the embassy to catch up on telexes. Ali tells us that Hanif is going to make us something fresh for supper.

Monday, November 5, 1990

AFTER OUR CANADIAN COFFEE MORNING for Dr Mahia Al Agaroush a few days earlier, she had told us of the anguish that Saudis like her feel at the American military presence here. She felt that it was necessary, I believe, but felt so badly that the "Arab nation was falling apart." She had wanted social change. She pointed to the fact that the Kingdom could ill afford to have half of its population — its women — under wraps (literally!). But there was great concern about whether there would be a modernizing trend or, instead, a dreadfully conservative reaction against the Westerners' social mores. People such as she believed that the Americans wouldn't leave.

At a party in our embassy's Wadi Club, I had a further interesting chat with Riyadh Aweida, the embassy's translator/press analyst. He had been in Jordan and Syria during the month following the invasion of Kuwait and noted a lot of popular support for Saddam Hussein in both those countries. A lot of people there say that the Western world watched Israel take over the West Bank and the Gaza Strip without lifting a finger. At that time and since then, Saddam had been strong in supporting the Palestinians. But now that he had taken action against the wealthy sheikhs of the oil-rich Gulf states, the West leaps into action. (President Bush insisted that there be no linkage between the two issues, but apparently that was not so easy to ignore.)

A deeply felt resentment of the imperialistic past persisted. One certainly cannot understand the Middle East without knowledge of its history and the role of the Western nations in drawing boundaries after the First World War. In fact, Saudi Arabia is about the only country in this region without a colonial past (at least since it lost lands to the Ottoman Empire).

Wednesday, November 14, 1990

THE VISIT OF BILL MC KNIGHT, our minister of national defence, was a success. Everyone at the embassy pitched in and worked very hard. Because of the Saudi officials, all the scenarios and precisely timed programs kept changing right up to the arrival of the eight-member delegation. The program, as it read on Saturday, provided for the minister to arrive at 7:30 p.m. on Tuesday, November 13. The minister agreed that a reception at the residence for a couple of hundred Canadians on his arrival would be very helpful. Then next day he would meet Minister of Defence Prince Sultan in Riyadh and have lunch with him. So Albert Galpin arranged to extend invitations to the Canadians.

But as preparations were being made on Sunday at midnight, we returned from a dinner party given by Singapore's chargé d'affaires. Word had come that Prince Sultan and King Fahd were in Jeddah and that the King would see Minister McKnight in his palace there on the Tuesday night of his arrival! So Albert and his gang contacted everyone to change the reception to Wednesday afternoon at 3! (It was probably a good test of our warden system for contacting people.)

They managed to reach everyone except Moe Cussen, who was already on his way from Jeddah, and the Benoits, the nice couple in Jubail, who had already left for Riyadh. I invited Moe in for a drink when he arrived at the door Tuesday evening. He is a pleasant chap who sells for Clorox. He came again next day for the real thing. We still haven't located the Benoits.

The minister and his officials met with Prince Sultan around 10 p.m. Tuesday to sign an air transport agreement, then went to see King Fahd, and arrived at the guest palace in the wee hours, exhausted after travelling from Ottawa to London, then to Jeddah.

Wednesday morning they flew in a Royal 737 to Riyadh. (Regulations gave the Canadians' pilots a 16-hour layover to rest. Pity no one allows the same humanitarian measures for the minister!) They were briefed by our American pal, General Olson, and then had a meeting with Crown Prince Abdullah. Then they called on Minister of Petroleum Hisham Nazer. Finally they came to the residence for the reception before leaving at 4:30 to fly on to Doha, where Larry Dickenson would take over.

Donald McLennan had worked till 2 in the morning. David Hutchings had been with Allan and the minister throughout, taking notes for telexes back to Ottawa. So everyone was very relieved when it was over, and the first ministerial visit in five years had been pretty useful.

Press coverage has been good. There was a press conference in our dining-room during the garden reception. Also, the television news offered five separate items, each with a full set of pictures! And no one taped it! The necessary technological know-how is beyond all these excellent diplomats. Don McLennan didn't see the news because he went to a violin and piano concert at our embassy after the minister's party left. There was a really good picture of him in Nazer's meeting. He'd love to send it to his daughter, Alyson, in Ottawa. So maybe he'll be able to get a copy from the TV station.

Allan has just been over to the office, and tells me that the religious police are cracking down in a big way. There was a party in one of the villas attached to the Sheraton Hotel last night, and the *mutawe'en* (literally, volunteers — religious police) arrived to arrest a bunch of Canadians, Americans, British, and Australians — about 20 in all. Andrew Shisko is on his way downtown to see if he can find out more. There are various kinds of tensions in the air these days. Fear of war, fear of social change, fear of foreign influence.

And then I can report a lovely, tranquil evening! We went over to the embassy for the third and last night of the concert. (Actually, we popped in to the reception at the Belgian embassy first. They were celebrating the 60th birthday, back on September 7, of their beloved King Baudouin.) Concerts, as well as theatre and other artistic endeavours, were not permitted in the Kingdom, but the embassy was designated 'Canadian territory,' so we allowed and even encouraged the diplomatic community to hold concerts in our atrium. The artists were two young Dutch brothers: Silvain Kroon, on violin, and Vincent, on piano. Their program of Mozart, Beethoven, and Brahms was thoroughly enjoyable. Even a modern piece by W. Pijper was pleasant to hear. It was a good change of pace, and we both enjoyed it. Colonel Clark Little, a Canadian working with the joint command, sat with us. He was recovering from the ministerial visit too.

Canadian military 'guests,' Wadi Club, Canadian embassy

CHAPTER 11

DRIVING MEN CRAZY

Tuesday, November 6, 1990

WE WERE AT NOLENE AND ABDULLAH AL DABBAGHS' last evening for a very pleasant dinner. Also present were Sir Alan and Lady (Grania) Munro (British ambassador and his wife) and Iman and Saleh Al Hegelan.

All conversation stopped when Iman announced: "Next week women are going to start *driving*!" Not, she went on to say, putting on a massed one-time demonstration, but simply beginning to drive to the supermarket, to schools, to offices, or anywhere they normally would have to be driven. This was exciting news indeed.

"We would like to have international press focus on this, so that the King will be too embarrassed to put a stop to it," Nolene declared. Foreign women could follow their lead, but should not try to show the way themselves.

During the dinner, Iman expressed the view — which other Saudis shared, she said — that the Gulf crisis is a plot by the

A light moment with Sir Alan Munro

American CIA to gain a foothold in the Middle East. She referred to a 1983 article that predicted this. She insisted that Saddam Hussein remained obstinately in Kuwait because he knew he was safe; he was in cahoots with the CIA. She saw Saudi Arabia as loser no matter what the outcome, and she feared that the United States would keep its troops in the Gulf. She, by the way, worked as a director in the all-women company — Al-Sharika Al-Khalijiah Lil Inmaa (Al-Khalijiah Development Company) — that Dr Aisha Al-Mana set up to train women to work in business.

The Aggads were at the dinner too. Allan says that Omar Aggad, the senior Palestinian Saudi living in the Kingdom, expects a positive outcome for Saudi Arabia. Nolene told me that a lot of Saudi businessmen feel frustration at receiving directives from the King without having any input in decision-making. Certainly, change seems to be in the air. The crisis has people worried, and their conversations are more serious and meaningful these days.

Friday, November 16, 1990

THE WOMEN DID DRIVE ABOUT A WEEK AGO. We heard about it next day by word of mouth, since these things don't get into the press here. (The *New York Times* and CNN covered it, however.) Apparently the women banded together to drive as a demonstration. There were 47 of them in several cars who gathered at the Tamimi-Safeway supermarket parking lot. They drove up and down streets from there until police picked them up and took them to the station, which detained them, some people say, until about 4 a.m. Their husbands were required to take them home with a promise to ensure that they do not do this again.

Since then, we have heard that ten women university professors were suspended, and that some supportive husbands had been fired from their positions. We hear, too, that the women involved will be prohibited from travelling abroad for two years or more. It is difficult to know how many of these items are rumours.

Gloria Al-Dorani, who writes for the *Riyadh Daily* and may be a friend of some of these women, told me about some protests at the women's university *against* the radicals. That is, some very conservative young women oppose this sort of change as anti-Islamic. So there seems to be quite a debate going on behind the scenes. I have been trying to reach Madiha Al Agaroush, but my telephone calls have not been returned. I'm worried that she is in big trouble. Possibly her husband, who is a liberal-minded professor, is suffering from the reaction too.

There was an item on the front page of the Saudi newspapers on November 14. People say it was featured on the television news too. The headline read: "Women Barred from Driving": "The Ministry of the Interior reiterated that all women are banned from driving cars, adding that deterrent penalties would be applied to anyone who violated this ban." Citing a *fatwa* (religious edict) from Sheikh Abdulaziz bin Baz, president of the Permanent Committee for Islamic Research and Issuing Fatwas, and other authorities, the statement said, "Women were outlawed from driving vehicles as it contradicted the right Islamic code of conduct ... The Ministry of the Interior drew the attention of the citizens and residents that this fatwa should be respected by all people in the Kingdom."

Today the Saudi Press Agency provided an article to all the local newspapers, which reports on Minister of the Interior Prince Naif's statement: "The total number of women who participated in the cavalcade did not exceed 47. This included those women who had lived abroad and received non-Islamic education." He suggested that their timing was all wrong, given the uncertainties of hostilities with Iraq. (He probably has a point there.)

All of this is interesting to follow. One worries, too, because the backlash could make life miserable for fresh, exuberant women like Aisha, Madiha, and the architect/designer whom my sister, Ruth, and I had met earlier in the autumn.

Saturday, November 17, 1990

I HAVE BEEN TRYING FOR SEVERAL DAYS to reach Madiha to invite her for lunch, along with Aisha, Saoud Al Dabbagh, Iman Al Hegelan, Mary Hutchings, Elvham Nasser, and Cathy Moreau. My phone calls are not returned. I wonder if this is related to the demonstration. Finally, I call Saoud. She says she has been trying to reach Madiha too. She says things are terribly difficult for the activists. "We're not able to talk about it at all," she tells me.

I won't try again to contact Madiha.

Saoud agreed to come for lunch, as did Iman. I decided not to ask Aisha this time because she may be at risk if it seems that there is a gathering of 'radicals' here. I hope Madiha is all right.

Tuesday, November 20, 1990

HAD A VERY PLEASANT LUNCHEON TODAY. There were six of us: Iman Al Hegelan, Cathy Moreau, Saoud Al Dabbagh, Mary Hutchings, Elvham Nasser, and me.

The three Saudi women had lots to say about the repressive reaction to the driving. Aisha Al-Mana, a leading figure in the event, but missing from this little gathering, has felt she should leave Riyadh and return to Dammam to be with her family. She feared that her women's company would suffer because of continuing harassment. Saoud said that the participants are not permitted to travel abroad for five to ten years. They all agreed that was the worst part of the punishment! They said phones are tapped; Saoud hasn't felt able to go to her store at Al Akariyah.

They were incensed at Prince Naif's blaming "Western-educated" women who turned their backs on Islam. They maintain that most of the women had not studied in the West, and anyway driving has nothing to do with Islam. Saoud says she comes from a very religious family and will take a back seat to no one regarding strength of religious conviction. In fact, she desperately hopes for social change so that she can continue to live here and practise her religion in accordance with her beliefs. Iman says that many people are beginning to say, "To hell with it; we might as well move out of the country!"

All of the women were upset to realize many women opposed change. Elvham, who teaches at the Institute of Public Administration, told of the backlash there. We had all heard about the same response at the university.

Rejoining the Workforce?

I WAS FINDING THE ROLE OF AMBASSADOR'S WIFE very satisfying, and the events of August made it even more timely, demanding, and fulfilling. But I had rejoined the labour force in the mid-1970s and was looking for some professional activities outside the embassy that would bring me into regular contact with the people around me.

I wondered what sort of skills would be portable — transferable whenever External Affairs moved Allan and me. An attractive possibility seemed to be teaching English as a foreign language (TEFL), which was certainly in demand in Riyadh. I inquired about the MEd program in TEFL that the Ontario Institute for Studies in Education (OISE) offered in Toronto. It seemed that I could take a course lasting two summers to complete the program. I suggested to Allan that I could live either on the boat in Pickering harbour or with our kids while taking the summer course in Toronto. He suggested I do the same thing in Britain, at the universities in Edinburgh, London, Oxford, or Cambridge.

Accordingly, in November 1990 I met with Malcolm Young at the British Council offices in Riyadh and asked him for literature about such courses. He promised to send material the next week.

Subsequently, I had a meeting with Mohammed Al Hazzah,

head of the Audio-Visual Department at the King Faisal Specialist Hospital, about another possibility. He was looking for a writer/ editor to produce its bi-weekly newsletter and to prepare scripts for video productions. He was a very likeable person, and I spent a stimulating hour with him.

The department's suite of offices is attractive, and all the elements of production are handled there. Al Hazzah needed someone with computer skills, writing ability, and experience with multi-media. I had all that, but he seemed surprised that I had no formal journalistic training. (Unfortunately, I couldn't find my tape of the video I made in the House of Commons to introduce new MPs to the vagaries of private members' business. I think he would have found it interesting.)

The hospital had in-house video channels very much like those in the House. They made video productions of seminars, interesting operations, and counselling of patients, and insisted on very high quality for export to the United States and Britain, as well as throughout the Kingdom. It all looked really interesting.

One major obstacle remained for me: the hours: 8 to 6! I suggested I would strongly prefer 8 to 1 because of all my embassy duties. Al Hazzah seemed intent on a full-time employee, to accommodate seminars and other special events whenever they occurred. Also, the production teams had deadlines and would need the writer/editor to be on call. Too bad, because it looked fascinating, and something I was sure I could do. Al Hazzah suggested that my experience would suit me for a position in the executive director's office. He asked if he might pass my résumé to him, and I agreed.

Driving Mrs Epp

DRIVING REMAINED FRAUGHT. Later, plans were under way for an official visit by Minister of Energy Jake Epp and his wife. They would bring along officials and business people too. I developed a program for Mrs Epp, with a plan to take her sightseeing: to the palaces at Al Diriyah and to the King Faisal Centre and the Tuwaiq Palace in the Diplomatic Quarter. I wanted to take her to the Institute of Public Administration too. She would enjoy seeing the lovely building and the very keen students.

So, bundled in our abayas, Mrs Epp and I sat in the back seat of the car ably driven by Atta on our way to the school. I think

Suitably attired, heading to the Institute of Public Administration to visit Nora's eager female students.

Allan with the Honourable Jake Epp and Lydia Epp

that Mrs Epp enjoyed meeting the young women in my class, and it was good experience for them to meet a Canadian associated (by marriage) with the Canadian government.

As we departed from the institute, however, we had an incident that provided a lesson to me to be more careful. We had, of course, removed our abayas for our visit in this all-female school. Upon leaving, we carried our abayas — my careless mistake! We entered our car, and, as we pulled out, the mutawe'en intervened and prevented our car from moving! Atta jumped out, moving the men away from us, and explained to them in Arabic what important guests he was transporting! It took several minutes, which seemed like hours, before these threatening religious police backed away. Whew!

PART FOUR

Resolution 678

(December 1990—Mid-January 1991)

Photo on previous page: U.S. National Security Council briefing, Camp David, Maryland, Saturday, January 19, 1991. From left: Chairman of the Joint Chiefs of Staff Colin Powell, Secretary of State James Baker, Secretary of Defense Dick Cheney, unidentified man, National Security Advisor Brent Scowcroft, President George H.W. Bush, unidentified man

CHAPTER 12

WARY CHRISTMAS
(1990)

Wednesday, December 5, 1990

ALLAN IS *EXTREMELY* BUSY. He has been very tired the last couple of days, and really shows the strain around his eyes. When he came home from the office yesterday afternoon, I tucked him into bed for a couple of hours. But the phone rang almost immediately, with Larry Dickenson calling from Bahrain to discuss the new advice to give Canadians and the possible arrival of a Canadian military attaché in the Gulf area. Apparently, concerns about terrorism are increasing in Egypt and Jordan as well as Saudi Arabia.

We have a man from the Canadian Security Intelligence Service (CSIS) here. Normally he is situated in Amman, Jordan, but he has come to meet Allan this morning and to go with him to sign an agreement re security/information matters with intelligence chief Prince Turki.

I am to leave here for the airport at noon today, to fly to Dammam, in the Eastern Province. Allan will be at the meeting with Prince Turki, so he will go to the airport separately; the men accompanying him will be driven back to the embassy. In all, Allan's assistant has had to arrange three cars to pull it off. Actually, a fourth one took Andrew Shisko to the airport earlier because he is 'advancing' the trip. One of our soldiers will go with me. He's going with us to Dammam too.

We'll be staying at Le Méridien Al Khobar, halfway between Dammam and Al Khobar. Dinner with the Canadian group will be at the Oberoi Hotel. We were supposed to be taken to the Aramco Exhibition this afternoon, but Allan thinks the day is already pretty full.

I expect that Allan will be announcing that he intends to have Andrew Shisko move to Dammam and run an office there until the crisis is over. I hope that Andrew's being on the spot will somewhat comfort the Canadians. He has been working very closely with them in developing the warden system for communication. I must admit that I don't envy him his moving closer to such a vulnerable area! In my view, everyone has had lots of time to analyse what has been going on.

With UN Resolution 678 (November 29) having spelled out clearly its deadline of January 15 for Iraq to withdraw from Kuwait, there is no reason for any sane person to stay in the Gulf area beyond Christmas. They should leave now while they can book a flight on a plane. In fact, KLM has just cancelled all flights to Jordan because of the high costs. No doubt similar announcements will follow soon. Our embassy Canadians are starting to book flights for their dependants just in case. (Administrative officer Heather Bracken, her husband, Michel, and their two children are in Canada now to finish off Heather's maternity leave and to celebrate Christmas; it's hard to know whether they should come back — they would probably be wise to stay in Canada longer.)

Wednesday, December 12, 1990

OUR TRIP TO DAMMAM SEEMED A GREAT SUCCESS. Corporal Alain LeClerc accompanied us. Andrew met us when we arrived and drove us immediately to the Aramco Exhibition, where organizers greeted us graciously and had arranged a guided tour by a very friendly Saudi. Pictures were being taken throughout the tour, so I anticipate receiving a commemorative photo album (like the one from the Royal Commission in Jubail).

The dinner took place in the dining-room of the Oberoi Hotel. Allan spoke to the hundred or so Canadians. When he announced a new office in Dammam, with Andrew and Alain in charge, you could feel the tension ease among the audience — people near me were nodding, smiling, looking quite relieved. Alain and Andrew both said afterwards that they, too, noticed the positive reaction. Roy Gunther-Smith, who had organized the

On the road to Dammam

event, told me that employees are pretty fed up with Aramco's approach and eager for any support we can provide. Apparently the oil giant is going to cancel family benefits for people whose dependants are away. Such threats sure don't help at this very difficult time. The firm is also very slow and bureaucratic about giving out passports and arranging exit visas.

There was a question-and-answer period after Allan's speech, which he handled very well. Roy said to me it was obvious that Allan had prepared well. I had been leery of this whole exercise because the people in this vulnerable region are very uncomfortable. Wives who had fled in August and stayed away for a couple of months are back now and reluctant to leave again, and the uncertainty tortures everyone. But finding morale so high was a pleasant surprise. I spoke to several people before and during dinner and grasped that they have freely chosen to live and work here: wonderful climate, interesting work, and excellent benefits make the risks seem manageable, so far. And surely they realize that they can arrange to leave. In fact, Roy Gunther-Smith tells me about two families leave Aramco each day, according to his wife, Norma, who works in personnel there.

Allan told the group that Ottawa still advises dependants to leave the Eastern Province — a policy currently under review. A new advisory will arrive in the next day or so (with instructions for dependants and non-essential workers to leave Riyadh as well). A long briefing by Colonel Clark Little, from the joint command, informed Allan to expect war soon.

Monday, December 17, 1990

WE HAD OUR CHRISTMAS PARTY for the embassy staff last night. This year there were 60 people, so we had the buffet dinner in the atrium after drinks in the residence. It worked better than we anticipated. With red tablecloths, a long buffet table decorated with poinsettias and red candles, and eight tables each with flowers, candles, and Christmas serviettes, it all looked very festive.

Hanif did a great job of organizing and preparing the food. We had a couple of turkeys, sweet potatoes, lasagna, cold eggplant, fish, green jello and red jello, salads, rolls, and so on. Each time I asked Hanif if he needed any help, he said that everything was under control ... and indeed it was. Desserts included a sponge apple cake, pumpkin pies, lemon pies, lemon mousse, plum pudding, mince tarts, and cookies. We all went back into the residence for coffee and Christmas carols.

Christmas, 1990

Some of the guests had gifts for us. Pablo (a gatekeeper) and his wife brought a clock installed in a violin. Joe Fakhri and his wife brought a poinsettia, and the Shiskos gave us a bouquet of yellow and white cut flowers. Murray and Amira Lewis gave us a crystal vase, which will be very useful for the flowers we bring in from the garden these days. A new receptionist, Mayada, and her dentist husband gave us an elaborate cake plate. Very kind of all these people. I wrote thank-you notes this morning early because I will be leaving this morning for Dammam.

I had told Ali that we should probably consider having only a cocktail party for the embassy staff next Christmas because there might be even more than sixty by that time — too much work for Hanif. But Hanif spoke to me about it this morning. He said he wants to do it again next year no matter how many people

Allan carves Christmas turkey for a military guest

we invite! He says that we are the only embassy that invites *all* its employees "big and little" to sit down together for dinner. All their buddies envy them and think they are so lucky because we are so nice! The waiters we hired to serve the dinner while our guys were guests thought it was all pretty special. So the A-team are willing to put the effort into it, and were very cheery and appreciative today, even while they were working at putting things away and cleaning up.

Wednesday, December 19, 1990

WE WENT TO A DELIGHTFUL DINNER at the American residence last evening. The new home looks wonderful, with its warm wood tones a charming background for masses of poinsettia wreaths and a beautiful big Christmas tree in the foyer. There were candles in lanterns, red ribbons, and gaily decorated tables for dinner. All very pleasant, as a refreshing pause during such a busy time.

During dinner, Chas Freeman (American ambassador) was telling me that he has flown to Jeddah for meetings with the King and princes 44 times since August 2. There is an armed forces aircraft that takes him, thank goodness, so he can return to Riyadh at 3 a.m. if necessary. (We all know the weird hours the Custodian of the Two Holy Mosques keeps!) He has had Secretary of State James Baker four times, a third of the 100-member U.S. Senate, a quarter of the 435 Representatives, and various cabinet secretaries. I don't know how he stays healthy.

Alan and Grania Munro (Britain) were there too. They have probably been equally busy with official visits. Prince Charles is to arrive in the next day or so, and Alan will attend Crown Prince Abdullah's luncheon for him on Friday.

Dr Roman Judzewitsch, an Australian endocrinologist at King Faisal Specialist Hospital and Research Centre and the Riyadh Armed Forces Hospital, both in Riyadh, sent me a novel by Gabriel Garcia Márquez, who won the Nobel Prize for literature in 1982. I've just begun to read it and expect to find it enjoyable. We had had a good chat at the Australian residence the other evening, and I had promised to send him our copy of Alice Munro's new short stories, *Friend of My Youth* (1990).

We called Jill in Toronto yesterday to wish her "Bon voyage" — she's leaving for British Columbia today. We also talked to David, who told us about all the painting, wallpaper removal, etc., that he and Siobhan are doing these days. They were going last night with Don Gibson, a colleague at McCarthy Tétrault, and his wife to view pictures by Denise Ireland, who also is wife of one of the lawyers at the firm. David is a young new lawyer who has a savings bond he has dubbed his 'art bond.' It has come due; he has $2,000 available for a purchase. He was really looking forward to buying one of Ireland's paintings because he has admired her work for quite some time.

Swam a mile today. After being away for two weeks, I had started back swimming by doing a half-mile a day with Allan for a week. I was alone today, so decided to increase 'the dose.'

Sunday, December 23, 1990

IT'S INCREDIBLE TO THINK that we are moving quietly but seemingly irrevocably toward war! Each day we read disquieting news items: for instance, that Iraq had a civil defence exercise yesterday that evacuated a million residents from the poorer sections of Baghdad. At the same time, Saddam Hussein has stated that

Riyadh's King Faisal Centre for Research and Islamic Studies

he will (not 'might') use chemical weapons if provoked. President Bush and new British prime minister John Major agree that war is likely. Canada is issuing today an advisory that dependants leave the Riyadh area as well as the Eastern Province (and Bahrain, Qatar, and other states as well). Even while the United States, Britain, and other nations were offering their support to King Fahd, the mission's credibility required Arab and other Muslim countries to join in as well. Egypt, Morocco, and Syria pitched in. Their involvement, along with that of states on the Indian subcontinent and in western Europe, Australia, and so on, would allow King Fahd to justify the mission to his people. Twice, the United Nations Security Council passed resolutions, finally posing a deadline of January 15, 1991, for Iraqi forces to withdraw from Kuwait.

U.S. Secretary of State James Baker was totally engaged in the diplomatic negotiations on behalf of President Bush. Everyone realized how crucial it was to persuade the Saudi people that the apparent meddling in their affairs was in their interest. Hence the focus on liberating Kuwait completely.

Our loyal A-teamers were becoming anxious. They feared that we would all leave. Would we take us with them to Canada? Should they go home to Pakistan? All three remained determined to stay.

It could be quite a conflagration in the Middle East. Turkey is sending thousands more troops to its border with Iraq. Belgium and other NATO forces will move into Turkey as reinforcements. Israel would likely get involved, and Jordan is certainly vulnerable to any aggression on that side, even though Syria has promised aid. The heads of the Gulf Cooperation Council (GCC) counties — Bahrain, Kuwait, Oman, Qatar, Saudi Arabia, and the United Arab Emirates (UAE) — are meeting now in Qatar. They realize that, regardless of war, they need new security measures. Headlines call for greater cooperation among the Gulf states.

I am most uneasy about the threat of chemical warfare (and biological too, I suppose). We have a certain number of suits at the embassy for *Canadian* personnel. I'll be darned if I can figure out how or why we can practise with this equipment when there is none for Ali, Hanif, and Zafar! When I question Allan, he says that we would send them home before we needed to use the stuff. But how do we know when that will be? The best plan I can figure out is to send them home as soon as the first shot is fired. But surely we may need them to help with evacuees or Canadians who may seek refuge here. If so, then surely we must give them the full drill. Perhaps that's the answer. (It helps to write this out, rather than have it go round and round in my mind.)

Tonight (Sunday 23rd) we are going to a black-tie Christmas Wassail at the British residence. Prince Charles is about, so maybe Alan Munro won't be able to attend his own party. We are getting too close to hostilities now to do too much more revelling, I think.

Last night we were at Teymour and Faisa Alirezas' for an intimate little dinner. That seems appropriate for the current situation; if we entertain in January, I think it should be dinners for 12 max. Alirezas included Abdullah and Nolene Dabbagh and Ahmed Al-Malek, as well as Rafael and Gabriella Steger (Mexico) and us. It was perfectly elegant. Their home is designed to reflect the indigenous culture in an attractive way. Faisa is very artistic herself, and their home is charming. It was a very pleasant evening.

I finished the book by Garcia Márquez and returned it to Roman Judzewitsch. It really was most enjoyable: lots of romantic description combined with unexpectedly realistic detail.

Currently I'm reading H.H. Stern's *Fundamental Concepts of Language Teaching*, on loan from Mary Hutchings, who teaches

English as a second language (ESL). We have a wonderful list of books to read: Mordecai Richler's *Solomon Gursky Was Here*, Victor Ostrovsky and Claire Hoy's *By Way of Deception: The Making and Unmaking of a Mossad Officer*, Andrew Cohen's *A Deal Undone: The Making and Breaking of the Meech Lake Accord*, which John gave me, and a bunch of books that are still wrapped and sitting under the Christmas tree. It really is great to have the time to read, swim, and generally enjoy doing what appeals most. The freedom is terrific — no babies to tend, no work schedule to adhere to. Everyone should have a sabbatical like mine!

We received nice letters from Christina Harttila (who is stuck in Finland because of the crisis) and the Gaarders, who are now posted in India. I want to write them as soon as I can tear myself away from the computer. (This is more fun.)

Allan has called a full staff meeting for 3 this afternoon. He'll tell them about the new advisory, adding that workers are expected to stay on the job. Subsequently he will also be having a meeting of wardens to pass along the new advice. Most people have been making plane reservations for the first week in January. In fact, the paper today reports that flights are filling up. The embassy has been tracking the availability of seats and will be able to keep the wardens informed.

The military aide assigned to the Canadian ambassador has said that none of the military personnel stationed here are feeling homesick about Christmas because it simply doesn't feel like that time of year. That's true. Even though we have the Christmas tree and poinsettias around, it still doesn't feel like Christmas. That's fine. We can enjoy having lunch in the sunshine on the lawn, and not dwell on the fact that we really are stuck to our commitments here. (I can't complain anyway, because I had Christmas with the family in Toronto on December 8.)

Sunday, December 30, 1990

LAST SUNDAY NIGHT WE WENT to the British Christmas wassail. It was a big bash with mostly British embassy staffers, British business people, Swedish Ambassador Lennart Alvin and his wife, Liss Karin, and us. The main attraction was a British military band in the garden. When we arrived, everyone was in the garden listening to the band. It was excellent! Apparently there are 19 such bands situated at the front with the troops. (The bandsmen double as stretcher-bearers!)

It was cold outside, so I was glad when we went in to sing carols accompanied by the piano. Everyone was given a song sheet, and people sang with more gusto than I've ever heard before. It was peculiar hearing all those familiar songs sung lustily by men with a British accent. In a Canadian setting it would sound affected, but, of course, with that group it was not.

There was a buffet supper, and people sat at round tables placed in rooms throughout the residence. This was the first party where children of our friends attended. They had just arrived for Christmas, and we would be seeing them throughout the holiday. The Munros' twin sons — Luke and James — were there.

Monday we went to the Alvins for their traditional Swedish family Christmas lunch. It was very pleasant. We were served *glugg* (mulled wine) when we arrived, and stood around in the living-room. (The Alvins have sent home their very beautiful art collection, because their government wasn't willing to assign it special insurance coverage during the crisis.)

Luncheon was a buffet with about six separate courses. I had to keep reminding myself not to pile food up on my plate for each course, even though it all looked delicious. We sat at tables in the sunshine in the garden, and it was very pleasant indeed.

Hard to realize it was Christmas in such agreeable surroundings outside. At my table, the 'host' was Hendrik, who is the Alvins' dear blond son in second-year university. Their daughter, Helena, looked after Allan's table. Both the kids were very hospitable and helpful in explaining the various foods we were to select for each course. Pat Freeman was there with their son, Nat, a very nice young man of about 23. The Cockings were there with their whole gang. (They had been at the wassail the night before too.) They had Joanna and Martin, who married a year ago; Celina and her boyfriend, William; Damion, who is 6 feet 3 inches at least and towers over everyone; and Jemima. who is a very poised young lady already at 18.

It was fun to get to know the families. I hope at least some of them will be here next year when our children come. I know they'd enjoy each other, even though our offspring are a bit older than most of these.

That evening, we went to a Christmas Eve party at Jennifer and Albert Galpins'. They had a houseful of nice young people,

Nicholas Cocking with Allan

and we enjoyed it very much.

When we returned home, we opened our gifts. Allan appreciated very much the silk tie from John and Abby, the Granatstein book about Trudeau's foreign policy from David and Siobhan, the book about Margaret Thatcher from Chris, and the crystal candlesticks from the Heembrocks. We were both also delighted to receive the money from Nana and Grandpa, and we're having fun deciding what we will buy with it.

Allan gave me a beautiful gold necklace. It is a Cartier design and will be a treasure all my life (and the life of my beneficiary some day). He also gave me a Casio digital diary, which is really a pocket computer. It can be downloaded to my IBM-compatible computer too. It is great fun. Already I have transferred all my telephone numbers and addresses to it, and have made shopping lists, etc. It has a great time-and-date system, which shows me what time it is in Ontario or any part of the world, as well as Riyadh.

Allan liked his briefcase. It had been wonderful in Toronto to go with David directly to the store where Siobhan had bought his briefcase, and to know which one I liked so much. I gave Allan books too, so we are going to really snuggle in on New Year's Day for some non-stop reading. *Insha'allah*.

Christmas Day (Tuesday) we went over to the home of Kate and Sean Kerwin, Irish diplomats. We didn't stay long because company was coming to our house. We had asked over for turkey dinner the Canadian military men who are guarding the embassy: Alain LeClerc, Luke Normore, Don McNeil, and a couple of others. Wayne House, whose wife remains teaching in Tokyo, came too. The men enjoyed the Christmas tree and the big dinner. Hanif got a kick out of the fact that they all had second helpings of the delicious shrimp bisque while Allan and I were talking on the phone to David and Siobhan.

On Boxing Day, we went to the Cockings' annual party. Again all the young adults were there with their parents. Thursday was free, except for my short meeting with a dozen women at the New Zealand residence to plan our various contributions to a New Year's Eve party there.

On Friday (28th), we went to a buffet luncheon at the home of J.P. and Laurel Floyd. They are a young Canadian couple who came here a few months ago. He trains pilots for British Aerospace and plays the trumpet in the Riyadh concert band. From there we joined up with a group that included the Alvins, the Cocking gang, the Munros, and General Sir Peter de la Billière (commander-in-chief of the British Forces in the Gulf) and his bodyguards, and we headed out into the desert for dinner. The Spanish ambassador and his wife, Dorly, rode with us in our Toyota four-wheel-drive. Allan was very pleased to find what a great

Jorge Tarud (Chile), Grania Munro, and Prince Abdullah,
at the prince's farm, December 28, 1990

vehicle it is in the sand. And he loved the compact-disc player in it. We listened to Ennio Morricone's exquisite score for *The Mission* (which Siobhan had given us) all the way there and back. Our evening on the desert was 'interesting.' We were going to the farm of our friend Prince Abdullah. On his farm, we and other diplomats walked some distance to see the Nejdi sheep and to choose one to be slaughtered for dinner. Then we visited a large group of camels. Prince Abdullah offered us some camel milk as it was taken from the mother. You should have seen old Allan and Lennart Alvin fade away to the background!

It was cold after the sun went down. We had drinks, then dinner standing around a big bonfire, and were home by about 11 o'clock.

Next day, Saturday 29th, was a workday for the embassy. In the evening we had 38 people for dinner. We had a Filipino chap who plays the piano with wonderful, mellow songs — perfect background music for the party. We had champagne and strawberries when guests arrived, then a buffet dinner that included boeuf bourgignon and spinach salad (my recipes), crab in crepes, smoked salmon, wild rice, stuffed zucchinis, cooked red cabbage, etc.

People sat at three large round tables in the dining-room, hall, and sunroom as well as on chesterfields. For dessert, the waiters served a really pretty poached pear with mincemeat filling — a recipe Hanif had found in a recent issue of *Gourmet Magazine*.

We had the Munro family, the Cockings, the Alvins, the Graces, with their son Andrew, who goes to Lakefield College (near Peterborough, Ontario), the Prices, the Cochranes (New Zealand) and their two daughters and their friend Meagan, as well as Commodore Ken Summers, who was here from Bahrain, Pekka Harttila (Finland), whose wife, Christina, and child remained in Finland because of the crisis, and Derek and Nadia Plumbly. Good party.

I felt sorry for the women at the party who were preparing

to leave Riyadh, along with their children, in case of war. Mary Hutchings had had such a dreadful time this autumn because of her sister's death and had returned to Riyadh in November. Now she finds that she and five-year-old John must leave again. She is very upset, and worries that John needs his Dad. Nadia Plumbly also has to leave. She has three small children. She and Mary both expressed the concern that, if they leave the country, their governments will be reluctant to allow them to come back for a very long time. Because of that, Nadia has decided to go to Jeddah, which they think out of reach of any chemical or biological attacks but still relatively close to Derek. Our people are thinking about doing that too. Mary and I are scheduled to fly to Jeddah on Wednesday to check out living accommodation.

I believe that either Pam, embassy secretary, or her husband, Colin Suter, will evacuate with the baby, and may go to Jeddah too. Heather Bracken, administrative officer due to return from maternity leave in Canada, proposes to establish her household in Jeddah. Her husband, Michel, may be able to engage in a project in the Jeddah area so that he could live there with the two children and the maid. Heather would come here to the office.

Diane Price, wife of a Canadian doctor, is leaving for Canada on January 5. Jennifer Galpin, Albert's wife, is expecting a baby around February 4 and could go to Jeddah and stay with Albert's brother there, but at the moment she seems determined to stay here. Linda Tiefenbruner, wife of Klaus, left for Canada with her two children the day after Christmas. The Bollmans are still away on holidays somewhere in Asia. Allan expects to contact them tomorrow; Bernadette and the girls will likely go to Paris to stay with Bernadette's family while Ron, our commercial counsellor, would return to Riyadh.

Today (Sunday 30th) I went, at the invitation of the King's wife and Princess Hussa, wife of Crown Prince Abdullah, to a program in support of the Kuwaitis. It was in the auditorium of the new Al Nahda charity building. Children sang patriotic songs and Kuwaiti women told about their experiences. There were a couple of short plays portraying the plight of the Kuwaiti families. Afterwards we bought some attractive crafts, with the proceeds to support the Kuwaiti cause.

Allan was at a luncheon the ambassador from Yemen gave today to open his new embassy — a great honour, because almost all the others there were Arab ambassadors.

We watched a film about the use of plastic suits to cover us in case of chemical warfare. Luke Normore, the sergeant responsible for these things, will give Allan and me a practice drill today. All suits are kept at the embassy, so I don't really expect to use one, since I wouldn't be able to go outside to walk over to the office. Our best bet here, I think, is to find a sealable room and stay there for a number of hours. I'll check with Luke to see which rooms are best for the A-team and me. (Perhaps a bathroom — no windows, and we could seal the single door with masking tape. Or perhaps the basement — again, no windows. The advice is: go upstairs if a chemical attack, and head downstairs for conventional bombs. Hmmmm.)

What a busy week! I haven't had a chance to write letters since last Sunday because all my energy has been used up in partying. It sounds awfully decadent. The only justification I can put forward is that it helps Allan do his job. Wherever we go, he is gathering and sharing information or just simply developing friendships that occasionally make it a lot easier for him to call on people to meet visiting ministers and officials or tell him something Ottawa ought to know.

CHAPTER 13

GAS MASKS *for* NEW YEAR
(1991)

Tuesday, January 1, 1991

NEW YEAR'S DAY. David called at 8:15 this morning. A friend of his from Onondaga Camp days had been over, they had gone out for dinner, and they were just having a glass of champagne to celebrate the New Year. It was so good to talk to him and to hear about their new home. David said he had received a Christmas card from the A-team (Ali, Hanif, and Zafar) and was very touched by it.

Allan has been working at the office. David Hutchings, Riyadh Oweida, and Colonel Clark Little are all working too because of the ministerial visit that begins on Saturday. Allan has an appointment to see Madani at the Foreign Office at 3 p.m. So today is a fairly normal workday.

The party last night at the New Zealand residence was really terrific. They kept it smaller this year — about 30 adults and perhaps 15 grown-up children. Dominique, the wife of the Chilean ambassador, is an interior decorator and had volunteered to decorate with the help of ambassadorial offspring. They did a splendid job. There were balloons filled with helium everywhere, streamers, etc. Each of us received a hat on arrival, and there were lots of noisemakers at midnight. I couldn't get over what a pleasure it is to spend so much time with a large group of really nice people who have become very good friends in only a year and a half. I think particularly of the Alvins and Cockings, of course, but also Gabriella and Rafael Steger (Mexico), Inge and Pietr (Belgium), Nolene and Abdullah Dabbagh, the Maolinis (Italy), and Dorly from Spain.

Later that week, the British surprised everyone by promising to deliver gas masks to all their nationals in the Gulf. It has made other people increasingly edgy. Allan had asked Ottawa to look into sending 6,000 masks for our people. But he feels that the British were foolish in their timing: they had so recently advised dependants to leave and now are saying, "but we'll provide you with this equipment if you stay." Nicholas says somebody in Whitehall is a 'wimp.'

It was only a few days later, however, that a Canadian Hercules aircraft loaded with the gas masks arrived. With them were two teams of military experts to fit each mask and teach its wearer how to use it.

Wardens notified all the Canadians living in Riyadh and the Eastern Province, where many worked in the oilfields close to Al Khobar, Dammam, and Dhahran. The concern was that Iraqi attackers would move along the Persian Gulf in their effort to take hold of such valuable Saudi territory. If such an invasion occurred, then people would surely escape towards Riyadh, which also would be vulnerable.

At the embassy in Riyadh, Allan designated the parking lot

within the gates for distribution of gas masks to all Canadians living in the city. For three days the whole area was filled with lines of people seeking the counsel of our fine experts. Each person had to show Canadian identification. Curiously, there were several women fully covered in hijab and abaya who proved their *bona fides*!

In three days, all Canadians in Riyadh received gas masks, and in the following two days all those in the Eastern Province as well, thanks to our Andrew Shisko's extraordinary efforts.

I'VE JUST BEGUN READING SCOTT TUROW'S second novel, *The Burden of Proof*, and am looking forward to getting back at it. *We don't have any social engagements today!*

Peter Gzowski's latest tome — *The Private Voice* — made for some very pleasant reading. It is based on diary entries that he made for about a year from June 1987 to June 1988. He was in his fifth year as the host at *Morningside* on CBC Radio at the time and was continuing to enjoy considerable popularity across the country. His show aired weekdays from 9 a.m. till noon. He had already published one or two volumes of *Morningside Papers*, in which he responds to letters from his legion of listeners and reflects on many of the issues that arise on his program.

Gzowski commented on the style of writing that he had learned while he was working for *Maclean's* magazine under the legendary Ralph Allen, beginning in the late 1950s. "Open with an anecdote," he said. Only when you are about halfway through the piece, he advised, do you finally complete the anecdote/story. Meanwhile you have to convince the reader of the importance of the issue and of the need for her to read on.

He compared his 'conservative' approach with that, for example, of the *New Yorker* magazine and contrasted it with the

'New Journalism' of Tom Wolfe. He touched on these issues very briefly, however. His point was that journalists of his ilk believe that they must report facts about which evidence exists and is verifiable. The 'New Journalism' allows a description of events that might have happened; it is sufficient that they be only symbolic of reality. Interesting.

In any event, inspired by Gzowski's journal, I decided to try to do more writing of my own. Living in Saudi Arabia provided a pretty unusual opportunity to record some interesting experiences.

Tomorrow I am to leave here about 6 in the morning for a flight to Jeddah with Mary Hutchings in search of homes for our people to go to next week.

Thursday, January 3, 1991

ALLAN IS STILL TRYING to finalize the program for Mary Collins, Canada's associate minister of defence. So far, Allan has arranged meetings for her with Abdullah Bishara, the Kuwaiti secretary-general of the Gulf Cooperation Council (GCC), and Generals Horner and Waller of the U.S. Central Command. Prince Sultan may not be available, but Allan would be content with her seeing Vice-Minister of Defence Prince Abdul Rahman bin Abdulaziz. She also is definitely going to meet with Prince Khalid bin Sultan, commander of the joint Arab forces. Efforts are still under way to arrange a session with Foreign Minister Prince Saud. All these guys are swamped with visiting dignitaries from so many countries keen to give visible evidence of their support. It's a wonder they have time to do anything else.

Mary Hutchings and I went to Jeddah yesterday, leaving here at 6:15 a.m. We had a good flight, and our man there, Mayez

Teriaky, met us when we arrived. He had a schedule of appointments ready for us, beginning with the Al Bilad Movenpick Hotel.

This turned out to be the best bet for our Canadian mothers and children to stay for a few weeks. The bungalows have one bedroom, a living-room, and a tiny kitchen. Prices include all the hotel's services and facilities. There is a nice pool where women and children may swim from 8 a.m. to 2 p.m. (This may be the only hotel that allows women to swim at all. Perhaps the King's son owning it allows such a courageous — or outrageous, depending on your point of view — stand.) It has a beautiful garden with children's play equipment in one corner and tennis courts.

Across the road (the Corniche) there is a beautiful beach along the Red Sea. Mary could envision going for long walks with John, collecting stones and seashells. If she weren't in such an unsettled state of mind, it would make a good holiday. However, I suspect she'll go home to her parents in Leamington, Ontario — very far from David, but more stable than even Jeddah, where people worry about threats from Yemenis and other types of terrorism. Allan has told staff members that they'll have to decide on their plans by Monday (January 7). In the meantime, plane tickets have been booked to Canada, and four bungalows have been reserved at Al Bilad in Jeddah.

We had also looked at flats at the Sheraton Hotel, but they were too slick for settling in with children. That new hotel would be OK for a grown-up holiday weekend, but lacked the cosyness a family needs. We also went to Al-Shatly Compound, which has dozens of two- and three-bedroom houses. It has a nursery school, doctors' offices, pharmacy, and grocery store, as well as two recreation clubs. But Mary and I both saw it as more of a place to settle permanently.

The Corniche, along the Red Sea, Jeddah

We arrived back in Riyadh in time for a dinner at the Mexican embassy. Allan is finishing one of the books I gave him for Christmas: *Trudeau and Our Times*, by Stephen Clarkson and (his wife) Christina McCall. He is enjoying it very much and intends to move immediately to the book John gave me: *A Deal Undone: The Making and Breaking of the Meech Lake Accord*, by Andrew Cohen. He considers it great good luck to have both at the same time, partly because they focus on constitutional moves — first by Trudeau, later by Mulroney.

Sunday, January 6, 1991

THE DINNER LAST NIGHT for Mary Collins seemed to be a great success. It was difficult to decide whether or not I should attend, because spouses were not invited. Mary Collins is, however, a buddy of mine from the time I worked in the House of Commons, and so it seemed appropriate for me to be there — in my own home, after all.

We had invited our friend Prince Abdullah, but he had phoned earlier in the day to cancel. In the event, Teymour Alireza was coming, so he asked Walib Binzagr, an influential Jeddah businessman, to come along with him. We still had a full table (with a few last-minute adjustments to the seating plan).

We placed Teymour Alireza on Mary Collins's right, even though there were generals and ambassadorial types who would be higher on the protocol list. He is such an entertaining, pleasant fellow, as well as a good source of information, being an active businessperson, that he was a good choice to sit beside her.

Beside me was her acting host — Prince Fahad bin Mohammad bin Abdulaziz. He proved an agreeable dinner partner. He is a former pilot who has expressed interest in the Challenger airplane, which Canada is marketing in Saudi Arabia. He is a high-level official in the Department of Defence. At the official meeting earlier in the day, there had been an exchange of gifts: Mary Collins proffering the usual book about Canada, and Prince Abdul Rahman presenting in exchange a brand-new *uzi*! Gasp!

On my left was General Charles ('Chuck') Horner, head of the U.S. Air Force in the Gulf. He has been here since August, is careful not to drink because his troops are not allowed to. His family lives at the base in South Carolina, and his wife plays the organ.

Also present were Nick Cocking; General Taylor, U.S. air attaché here; Admiral Charles Thomas, assistant chief of defence

Allan greets Sheik Teymour Alireza.

staff for Canada, travelling with the minister; Commodore Ken Summers, commanding Operation Friction; and various other colonels and staff members. Abdullah Dabbagh, secretary-general of the Saudi Chambers of Commerce, came too. We had 22 people all at the table — the maximum possible.

Today we postponed a noon-hour luncheon because of a change in the schedule of meetings, so it will be combined with the press briefing at 3 p.m. They will be a hungry lot by then!

Some guests and some reporters arrived at 2:45, but I entertained them until Albert and Donald arrived to handle the press. Allan and the visiting delegation floated in shortly after 3. We had planned to have the press conference in the sunroom while the others had drinks and food in the living-room. But the TV cameraman said that there were too many windows, so we positioned the press and cameras at the far end of the living-room.

When the minister was ready, we invited non-press guests into the dining-room to help themselves to quiches and salad while the business went on in the living-room. All very complicated, but it worked. As usual, Ali and Hanif and Zafar organized everything very well. The minister's group left about 4:30, and Allan was back shortly to rest for a few minutes before having Andrew Robinson, director of political affairs for the Middle East Division of External Affairs, over for a working dinner with David Hutchings and Donald McLennan.

I went to the Algerian residence for a farewell dinner for the Moroccan ambassador's wife. This was a French/Arabic dinner — one of the advantages of representing a bilingual nation. Many ladies sat in large chairs and chesterfields for an hour or more, chatting desperately. Actually, I sort of enjoyed a visit with the older wife of the Nigerian ambassador. She tells me he is not a career diplomat but rather a university professor, so this is an unusual experience for her too. I also talked to a woman who is originally Syrian, married an Algerian, and has been in Saudi Arabia for more than ten years. She's leaving this week with her small child.

Monday, January 7, 1991

I SUPERVISED AN ENTRANCE EXAM for Lakefield College for Lina Somait. She is in grade 8 in a Saudi school and hopes to go to Lakefield next year. Her brother, Khalid, is already there. Meanwhile, Allan is at King Faisal Specialist Hospital speaking about government emergency plans. He is wound up pretty tight these days and is looking forward to being in tonight (the only evening all week).

Friday, January 11, 1991

WE HAD THE PRESIDENT of Canada's Urban Transportation Development Corporation (UTDC), David Pettenden, and his aide, Dan, for dinner last night. They are here for only a couple of days. Allan is having a luncheon for ten on Saturday to further their effort to sell trucks to the Saudi military. Pettenden said he is carrying with him a little kit including gas mask. He says he is concerned about terrorism and intends to cut back on his frequent plane travel for a while.

I am studying two books at the moment — *Fundamental Concepts of Language Teaching* (1983), by H.H. Stern, and the 13th edition of *The Chicago Manual of Style* (1982). I'm using the former to prepare for possible teaching; the latter, for potential work as a copyeditor.

I am also reading *One Hundred Years of Solitude* by Gabriel Garcia Márquez. I had enjoyed another book by the same author when Roman Judzewitsch lent it to me, and was glad to receive this novel from him the other day. (He and his wife and children, by the way, have left by now for Australia because of the crisis.)

And also on my list is Naguib Mahfouz, the Egyptian Nobel laureate, who is hailed as the originator of the modern Arab novel. (Arabic poetry has been flourishing for thousands of years. Storytelling may have been by word of mouth around campfires for many generations.) Mahfouz writes very depressing stuff — feelings of uselessness and desperation amongst bureaucrats dismissed after Nasser's Egyptian revolution of 1952.

I've also been reading Graeme Greene, having heard about him all my life and feeling guilty about not reading his books. Everyone has probably read *Our Man in Havana*. I hadn't; but I bet it's entertaining. I have read *The Power and the Glory* — wonderful. And, as I reported to the family, I was about to read his recent novel *The Tenth Man*.

Saturday, January 12, 1991

UN SECRETARY-GENERAL JAVIER PÉREZ DE CUÉLLAR is in Baghdad in a last attempt to avert war. He has met French President François Mitterrand and European foreign ministers as well as King Hussein of Jordan. They are offering a peace force and a Middle East conference — which may be difficult for the United States to accept. The deadline may blur, threatening the integrity of the multinational coalition. Saddam Hussein is a clever rascal.

Our embassy is well prepared to handle any emergency. The Crisis Task Force meets daily to handle any changes in advice to Canadians, information to the press, security precautions, measures of defence preparedness, and all other forms of communication between Ottawa and the Saudi government.

Canada's fighter planes are stationed in Doha, Qatar. Personnel from the Royal Canadian Air Force are also assigned to work at the Control Centre in the Saudi Air Force building in Riyadh, which controls all flights in the region.

We drove by the airport one day. I was astonished to observe air tankers on the ground as far as we could see.

U.S. Air Force F-16A Fighting Falcon, F-15C Eagle, and
F-15E Strike Eagle fighter aircraft fly over burning oilfield sites
in Kuwait during Operation Desert Storm.

PART FIVE

Tales *from the* Scud Café
(January 16—February 28, 1991)

U.S. Secretary of State James Baker

CHAPTER 14

MEMORIES *of* MRS MINIVER

(January 17–20, 1991)

Thursday, January 10, 1991

WELL, THE IMPORTANT MEETING in Geneva between U.S. Secretary of State James Baker and Iraqi Foreign Minister Tariq Aziz has failed. Allan and I, and the other guests, were just pulling back our chairs from the dining table at the Turkish residence when Baker's live, televised press conference appeared on Saudi Television. (This was a first for the Saudis to use a feed from CNN.) Worry etched lines in the haggard faces of those gathered round us. I watched the ambassadors from Yemen and Jordan, both of whose countries were supportive of Iraq. They must have felt uncomfortable among the rest of us. What would happen now?

Returning home to the Canadian residence, I listened to BBC shortwave radio. President Mitterrand of France seemed willing to intervene if an opportunity should arise. Western diplomats were leaving Baghdad. James Baker was on his way to Saudi Arabia.

I met with Sergeant Luke Normore, a fresh-faced Newfoundlander, who seems very competent, as well as cheerful and pleasant to have with us as protection. "Would you, with your military experience, review what we have on hand and list additional supplies we should get in case of emergency?" was my urgent plea. So Luke provided the information, and Hanif bought another 2,000 riyals ($650) worth of groceries for the residence. We'd be ready.

Thursday, January 17, 1991

IT WAS 10 IN THE EVENING of Wednesday, January 16, when Canadian Colonel Clark Little in Central Command (speaking discreetly on the insecure phone line) informed Allan that the coalition attack was imminent. The Embassy Emergency Team gathered in Allan's boardroom, which had communication facilities. I brought over coffee and cookies. The A-team stayed at the chancery to sleep in the drivers' room near the kitchen and the basement.

By 1 a.m. nothing had happened, despite some calls from Canadian press people saying they understood something was up. We were just coming out of the embassy to go home for some rest at 1:25 a.m. when we heard and saw the coalition aerial tankers flying overhead. This was the first wave on its way towards Kuwait.

At 3 o'clock Ottawa called: "The blizzard has begun." The U.S. ambassador phoned to report Saudi radar sites bombed at 2:40 and missile sites at 3. At 3:25 the air-raid sirens sounded in Riyadh.

President George Bush spoke on television. Afterwards, everyone was hungry, as well as under lots of stress, so Allan asked the A-team to go back to the residence to prepare a hearty breakfast for two shifts of people. Scrambled eggs, toast, jam, and coffee rarely tasted so good!

Returning to the embassy, Sergeant Luke Normore explained to all of us that we should carry our gas masks wherever we went. Further, we should practise till we could have them in place in nine seconds. He quietly passed out additional equipment — suits to cover our whole bodies, tape to attach to our clothing to identify gases in the air, and a 'mitt' with powder to apply to body parts exposed before total cover-up.

It was then that the realization struck me like a slap in the face: diplomacy had failed. We were at war.

The Canadian cabinet, after an all-day session, agreed to establish jointly with the British a field hospital behind the front lines (Operation Scalpel, within Canada's more comprehensive

Sergeant Luke Normore

Operation Friction). Five hundred medical military personnel from 1 Canadian Field Hospital in Petawawa, Ontario, were to set up a facility at Al-Qaysumah, near the front.

It was to make the announcement at 10 a.m. Ottawa time on Friday. At about that time, Allan received a call from the Department of National Defence (DND) in Ottawa saying that the announcement was being delayed 72 hours. Allan, however, had already spoken to Prince Saud's people and had, on instruction from Louis Delvoie, assistant deputy minister in Ottawa, sent a letter to the Saudi Ministry of Foreign Affairs and Department of Defence. Ah well, we'll see what happens next. Ottawa did announce at a press conference its plans to send six more fighter planes. Chief of Defence Staff John de Chastelain made that announcement.

Friday, January 18, 1991

A CALL FROM THE EMBASSY woke us about 4 a.m. There had been an Iraqi missile attack on Israel and reports about possible attacks on Saudi Arabia. Ambassador Larry Dickenson called at the same time from Bahrain to say that the sirens had sounded there and that the people there had donned their protective coverings and gas masks.

Larry called again to tell us about a major explosion and wondered if it had taken place in the Eastern Province. Allan and I dressed immediately, and Allan went to the office, where he was able eventually to contact Andrew Shisko in Dhahran. Andrew reported jubilantly that the Patriot missile had exploded an incoming Scud missile.

During the night there were several alarms in Dhahran, and Andrew and his group were able to go repeatedly to a bomb shelter. In the meantime, his military assistants have been asked by a couple of Saudi institutions to brief their people about the use of the gas masks; they are glad to be able to help.

The doors of our residence are locked for security, and curtains are pulled to protect us from possible shattering glass. A military guard comes by regularly to check. I stepped outside for a few minutes this morning and was surprised to find a beautiful sunny day with a mild breeze and birds singing.

It is 7:30 p.m. Allan is at the embassy, but hopes to come home in time to go to bed early. It may be an upsetting night if Iraq sends more missiles to Saudi Arabia and to Israel. Apparently the coalition planes are trying to get rid of mobile Scud launchers but so far report having blown up only six of 20, 40, or even 60.

On the night the war began — all aerial activity was now military — air tankers filled the sky above our embassy, heading for Kuwait. We had been seeing them for months lined up at the airport — carriers of fuel for airborne fighter planes. Now, as I watched and listened, they reminded me of a scene from William Wyler's film *Mrs. Miniver* (1942) where Greer Garson, in the title role, looks up to see dozens of Royal Air Force planes flying over England, protecting their country from German invasion.

Saturday, January 19, 1991

9:15 A.M. TEL AVIV has just sustained another missile attack from Iraq. This is the second. The first took place night before last. Israel has been very restrained and has not retaliated so far. But everyone believes that it will now have to respond. If it does, Jordan will likely be involved. This may affect the military coalition too, because Syria, for example, might have grave difficulty fighting alongside Israel.

We had a full night's sleep and awoke feeling very much better. Perhaps now is a good time to review what has happened in slightly more detail. We have been very glad, by the way, to have had installed only a few days ago a TV dish that receives the American TV networks CNN and ABC through the U.S. Armed Forces base in Vincenza, Italy. The coverage has been really amazing.

Allan phoned Klaus at the embassy and advised him to contact Ron, David, Don, and Albert for a meeting of the Emergency Task Force. They gathered together in Allan's boardroom, where telephones and other communication facilities are set up.

Sunday, January 20, 1991

THURSDAY (17ᵀᴴ) IS ALREADY A BLUR FOR ME. I tried to catch some rest during the day, but was feeling so enormously stressed that I couldn't sleep even after a bath. At noon Hanif made a huge platter of sandwiches for people at the embassy. He sent over a carrot cake and cookies as well. Thursday evening David Hutchings and Norma Shearer (Allan's secretary) came over for a supper of lasagna before returning to their posts.

Albert had faxed Ottawa on Tuesday, January 15, with the lists of Canadians in Riyadh, the Eastern Province, Jeddah and environs, Oman, and the United Arab Emirates. These lists seem to have helped officials in Ottawa who receive phone calls from anxious relatives.

Early in the day of the 16ᵗʰ, Margaret Shisko phoned all the wardens to give them the first message from the embassy: to stay home until further notice. She also asked them to do a final check on the names and numbers of people in each family. During the distribution of gas masks on Tuesday and Wednesday there had also been a check against our lists. So Albert was able to send a message yesterday to Ottawa to the following effect:

Saudi Arabia Total 3030:
> *Riyadh — 1516;*
> *Western/Jeddah Region — 985;*
> *Eastern Province — 539;*
> *United Arab Emirates — 1068;*
> *Yemen — 98;*
> *Oman — 165.*

Embassy has accounted for 4,361 persons in our area of consular responsibility. Events permitting, we will be adding changes to our computer database and will forward clean copy in due course.

Of 539 Canadians in the Eastern Province, 355 or 66 percent of the community were issued gas masks — a higher percentage if you exclude from the calculations children for whom no masks were available. In Riyadh approximately 800 masks or nearly 60 percent of the Canadian community were issued gas masks — we estimate that approximately 75 percent of the adult Canadian population were issued gas masks when taking into consideration that many more children remain in the Riyadh area, whereas in Eastern Province many more children have left.

Albert Galpin's consular team had done an excellent job of organizing everything. Andrew Shisko, assisted by Alain LeClerc and two other military personnel who arrived with the masks, organized gas-mask distribution for the Eastern Province. Elie Martel, a locally engaged person from the embassy, is with Andrew as well. They are doing great work in extremely trying circumstances. Margaret, Andrew's wife, is being very brave and uncomplaining here too. She must be very worried about Andrew.

Allan spoke last night to Marc Perron, Canadian assistant deputy minister for the Middle East at External Affairs. Allan suggested Ottawa extend some words of encouragement, along with some information about 'danger pay,' no doubt essential for our people in this time of war. Allan felt it would boost morale if Ottawa moved promptly rather than waiting till our guys started asking about it. Marc agreed.

Allan, accompanied by Luke for security, went downtown to the barber at the Al Khozama Hotel this morning. The barber, however, did not show up. I imagine it was kind of nice for Allan to have a little outing. One feels very much a prisoner of security and caution during such a tense time.

There is no mail coming in because airports are being used exclusively for military purposes. Yesterday we sent a short note by fax to each of our four children and to Allan's sister, Anne, in reply to the letter that she had faxed to us on the night of the first coalition attacks.

CNN reported that the American embassy had been evacuated during the night by military helicopter. There were fears about terrorism.

Meanwhile, Dorly, wife of the Spanish ambassador, has just called to invite me to her place for a game of bridge with her, Turkey, and Denmark!

I gave embassy secretary Pam Saunders a call today. She and the baby and the maid are staying in a little bungalow at the Al Bilad Hotel in Jeddah. She is glad she made the decision to go to Jeddah, where she doesn't feel so far away from her husband, Colin Suter, as she would in Newfoundland. There are no planes leaving Jeddah, so she is stuck there, but it still seems safer there than here.

CHAPTER 15

Bombs *over* Riyadh
(January 21–31, 1991)

Monday, January 21, 1991

L AST NIGHT WAS EVENTFUL. We had just settled into bed when the sirens sounded the first time. Everyone gathered at the embassy, but we shortly found that it was a false alarm. The A-team had just gone back to the residence when Allan's niece Lisa called from Canada to see if we were OK. We were still at the embassy while Allan reported to Ottawa, so I had a good little chat with her there.

We were asleep in bed when the second alarm sounded near midnight. So quickly we assembled again in Room B7 of the embassy. All of us wore gas masks, while the military chaps scouted around the building and checked with civil defence. When the all-clear signal sounded, most people went upstairs. I went home, but it was just a few minutes before the third siren indicated an attack. Again we were in our gas masks, while Patriot anti-missile missiles managed to intercept three or four incoming Scud missiles. (Iraqi aim doesn't seem to be too bad.)

Jennifer Galpin, almost fully nine months pregnant, remains calm throughout all this. She says the baby had hiccoughs during the last raid! Allan is glad the other mothers and children had left Riyadh in good time. I talked yesterday to Mary Hutchings in Leamington, Linda Tiefenbruner in Owen Sound, and Pam Saunders in Jeddah. Bernadette Bollman is still waiting in France, but she will probably leave soon for Canada, since the situation here is not improving.

Margaret Shisko and Klaus Tiefenbruner, an administrative assistant from the embassy, are coming for supper, along with Pam Saunders's husband, Colin Suter. (*Insha'allah*).

On Wednesday Don McLennan is going to Dhahran so Andrew can have a couple of days of leave.

According to a U.S. Pentagon source interviewed on BBC shortwave this morning, Iraq is going for "maximum psychological effect" — something that Allan has long thought would mean attacking Riyadh. The U.S. Patriot missile appears to be our 'hero-weapon.'

Tuesday, January 22, 1991

AT ABOUT 4:30 THIS MORNING, as we sat in our shelter in the embassy basement, someone asked what day it was. After a pause to reflect, I was able to say, "It's Allan's birthday."

As far as I know, at that moment there were two Scud missiles heading towards Riyadh during that attack. A Patriot missile intercepted one; in fact, we heard a big bang before we reached the shelter when that happened. The other got through and shattered windows. We haven't heard if there were casualties. Apparently there were 12 people injured the night before.

The sirens sounded again shortly after 7 a.m. We have just returned from that sojourn in Room B7 and haven't heard reports. CNN news is reporting attacks but is now not saying where in Saudi Arabia they are landing. That's probably very wise. Let's not let the Iraqi forces know exactly how their efforts work out.

Commiserated with the Indonesian ambassador's wife this morning. Rose Ali (Singapore) and the children (she told me) had left on January 16 at the insistence of their government.

Wednesday, January 23, 1991

TALKED TO ALL THE FAMILY YESTERDAY. My sister Ruth called about 4 o'clock. I had gone swimming. I had such a stomach ache that I thought it best to get some exercise, even though I didn't feel very safe being outside for a long time. I called her when I returned to the house. She said John and David have been very good at calling her as soon as they have reports from External Affairs saying we are fine after the latest attack.

During the evening John arranged a conference call with David, Chris, Jill, and Nana. They had a good chat with Allan to wish him "Happy birthday." It's so good to be in such close touch with them. It really is comforting. Allan received a birthday fax from his sister Anne too.

We had Canadian journalists for supper last night. They came after the briefing with the American officers in Central Command. Paul Koring writes for the *Globe and Mail*. A friend of Donald McLennan's has been faxing Paul's articles to the embassy; it is interesting to read a Canadian's impressions of Saudi Arabia and all that is happening here. Geneviève Garon is with *Radio-Canada* and *Téléjournal*. She is a young woman who has covered the House of Commons and, most recently, Latin America. There was also a man from Southam News.

All of us were expecting a busy night, with Scud missiles arriving at odd hours. As it turned out, we were spared last night. But Tel Aviv was hit in a heavily populated area. Koring was mentioning that Riyadh is just as close to missile sites in Iraq as Tel Aviv is. I had always thought we were a bit farther away. Anyway, we have found that the Scuds can certainly travel this distance, and they are terrifying. The experts still say that militarily they are of minor significance: they have to fall right on you to do damage. Chances are that most of us will emerge unscathed.

So we had a good night's rest. I swam half a mile this morning. During the lengths I do on my back, I watch the plane activity overhead; during the breaststroke lengths, I keep my head above the water to listen for sirens. Very relaxing.

Allan didn't take the time to swim this morning because he wanted to be sure to be at the office to say good-bye to Donald McLennan, who is going to Dhahran today to replace Andrew Shisko for a couple of days. It will be a much-needed rest for Andrew and a big relief for Margaret to have him here. Allan has appointed Dave Clark to be Donald's liaison with the embassy while he is in the Eastern Province. That way Allan won't have to receive the dozens of calls Donald is sure to make.

Jennifer continues to handle the stress magnificently. When she was here for supper last night I took her upstairs to see where the guest room is. Since she spends the days at the embassy, she might want to pop over here for a break or rest or whatever. So far she says she is doing fine. She has the office, which will be filled by Colonel Mel McLeod, the new military attaché, and has set up her sewing machine and made a comfortable bed for naps. Currently she is working on a quilt for the baby's bed.

Allan received a very nice fax from Belle Shenkman, a cultural impresario and pal from his days in London in the early 1980s, and her husband, Major-General Desmond Smith (he had been adjutant general of the Canadian army during the Diefenbaker years but, according to our understanding, had resigned in protest of the cancellation of the AVRO Arrow). Belle said that she and Des were thinking about us constantly. She concluded by saying: "As Canadians, we know that we have our finest representatives on this terrifying job at the right time." It is so encouraging to receive supportive messages like that.

I have written a one-page letter to Belle and Des, and one to our son John. Allan will fax them this afternoon, so they will have them in the morning (their time). John said on the phone that he really liked to receive them, so I'll try to keep doing it as long as this crisis goes on.

There is an ad in this morning's *Arab News*: "The U.S. Government is soliciting bids for the provision of guard services at the U.S. Embassy in Riyadh." Mon Dieu! They would have to offer a lot of money to entice someone to do that job!

I talked to Cathy Moreau (wife of a Canadian doctor here in Riyadh) this morning. She and Carol had decided finally to leave the Kingdom on Thursday. They had been planning to spend a few days in London and then go to Switzerland to ski and look at private schools. Alas, they were too late. It would have been a great holiday.

Cathy said that they have been using two bedrooms as safe havens during the Scud attacks. However, since the Iraqis have not used chemicals so far, they wonder if they should be on a lower level to avoid injury from an explosive impact. Since their house in the King Faisal Hospital compound has no basement, they have fixed up their dining-room with a mattress against the window and arranged the dining-room table so they could crawl underneath.

The hospital has got its act together. It has an in-house television service that broadcasts when the alarm goes off and advises when the alert is over. This helps, because it is not always possible to hear the civil defence alarm.

Thursday, January 24, 1991

THE U.S. GOVERNMENT has agreed to evacuate Canadians from Dammam in its military planes going to Spain, Frankfurt, or some other place (it keeps the destination secret). Wardens in the Eastern Province were contacted about this by 5 p.m. yesterday. By 9 p.m. there were 40 people scheduled to depart early this morning. This will relieve a lot of people. Another plane will leave on Saturday morning. It will be interesting to hear how many sign up for that.

Apparently the trip is not the most comfortable. It has canvas chairs for an eight-hour flight! A potty in the corner sports a curtain around it for a little privacy. And it costs about 50 per cent more than ordinary flights. No doubt, however, if people are really scared, it will be worth it.

A telex from Ottawa this morning reports that the Americans are considering arranging similar flights from Riyadh and that Canadians could sign on too. That's great news. It really provides the penultimate service for Canadians. The next step would be total evacuation, but only if there were a bunch of Scuds bearing chemicals. Or maybe if the Iraqis damaged facilities such as desalination plants. Anyway, current plans seem entirely appropriate for the level of hostilities at this time.

We had a flood in the drivers' room on the main floor today. The maintenance men were repairing a toilet and broke a water pipe. They were a bit slow in turning off the main water supply.

Allan called from the office to say that Commodore Ken Summers is coming to Riyadh tomorrow for meetings at Central Command. He'll have lunch with us. I was sorry to have to tell Hanif that the A-team would have to work on Friday (their holy day). They seem tired. Sleep is interrupted these nights.

Speaking of which, I forgot to mention that we did have an alert last night around 11:30. A CBC reporter from Calgary called Allan just as the siren was sounding, so the receptionist at the embassy had to advise him to call later: "The ambassador is on his way to the shelter." It was some time after 1:30 a.m. when the interview ended, and we settled back into bed.

Friday, January 25, 1991

I SWAM A MILE THIS MORNING. I think it really helps. The weather is absolutely wonderful.

Commodore Summers has just flown in from Bahrain and is here to meet with Allan over lunch before he goes to a 2-o'clock meeting with Central Command. Colonel Clark Little, the Canadian liaison with the coalition forces here in Riyadh, is with him.

There was absolutely no Scud missile activity during the night, so everyone probably had a pretty good sleep. (I have been going to bed with most of my clothes on so that I can reach the shelter quickly when the alarms sound.)

I have decided not to watch TV today, for a while anyway. There certainly is such a thing as war-information overload. I have been trying to concentrate instead on reading newspapers (which have been flown in from Jeddah for the first time since the war began). In the *Saudi Gazette*, a reporter tells of the "massive explosions heard near our flat in Sulaimaniya" (near the Al Akariyah souk shopping centre); the daylight hours may be "our own," but "the sleepless nights and the constant high state of anxiety is evident on faces of persons who are now just marionettes in a campaign of terror."

Michael Field, whose book about doing business in the Middle East we have read (*The Merchants*), reports now that Saudis, who never really expected war, are hardening in their resolve and are perhaps increasingly supportive of the royal family. At last, some political analysis to take one's mind off the next few hours!

Saturday, January 26, 1991

THREE ALARMS LAST NIGHT: 10:30 p.m., 3 a.m., and about 5 a.m. According to reports, Patriots intercepted two missiles, but there was considerable damage to an office building and some people were killed and several injured.

I phoned Kohinoor Dastgir (wife of the Bangladeshi ambassador) this morning. She said India and Sri Lanka (my short-hand for the ambassadors' wives) were on their way over, and she suggested I come too. So I popped in for about an hour. It felt good to get out. This was the first time I had been out of the Diplomatic Quarter since the war began. Streets were relatively empty, and there were numerous roadblocks for security checks of the few people out and about.

Dieta Van Es (whose husband heads the Saudi Hollandi Bank in Riyadh) called to chat just after lunch. I guess people are starting to want to talk to each other a bit more.

Allan sent a message from the office around 2 o'clock: the water pipe to the Diplomatic Quarter has broken, water would run out in about an hour, and repairs would take 12 to 24 hours. I filled the two bathtubs with water for flushing toilets.

Sunday, January 27, 1991

PLAYED BRIDGE AT DANISH RESIDENCE with Dorly, Fatima, and Nouran again. Not so much fun. I think I had too much coffee; felt uneasy.

Anna Cocking phoned to thank me for the cake I sent yesterday for British soldiers at the front and to ask for another to send on Tuesday. She also invited us for a very informal supper tomorrow evening.

Dieta Van Es called to invite us for lunch on Friday. She said she's ordering Chinese food because it's the easiest to cancel if need be.

We had only one attack last evening. A couple of Scuds arrived about 10:45 p.m. Reports say that Patriot missiles intercepted both, and I did see the Patriots in the sky as I ran over to the embassy. However, there was an explosion and lots of smoke. It is hard to tell how accurate reports are. Either the Saudis or their armed forces could be keeping secrets or even disseminating disinformation for Iraqi consumption.

Albert prepared a report for Ottawa this morning summarizing Scud attacks on Saudi Arabia. He said that since the Iraqis increased hostilities they have fired as many as 29 Scuds — 15 at the Eastern Province and 14 at Riyadh. The Eastern Province has reported no damage or deaths or injuries. In the Riyadh area, however, at least three Scuds appear to have penetrated the Patriot (anti-missile missile) defence system, injuring about 43 people and killing as many as six. Other embassies, in particular New Zealand and Australia, are considering an "organized departure."

Albert adds that all the attacks around Riyadh seem to be near the airbase or downtown, which indicates surprising accuracy, considering the 400 kilometres to the Iraq—Kuwait border.

Embassy officers visited the impact site in Riyadh of the January 21 Scud, next to a local insurance building, which also housed an appliance repair shop. The building was directly opposite the Riyadh Airbase, and only 500 metres from a row of U.S.—Saudi airborne early-warning and control (AWAC) aircraft, from Boeing, parked on the tarmac. The crater was approximately four feet deep and eight feet wide. The insurance building suffered heavy structural damage, with portions of the back buckling inward. The impact had forced heavy metal barriers in front of the building out of their frames, collapsed the second floor, blown out all the inside partitions, and tossed furniture and heavy appliances around. Buildings within a three-block radius had windows blown in, and, nearer the site of impact, window and doorframes were wrenched from walls. There did not appear to be any burn marks, possibly confirming the theory that the Scud may have been intercepted or exploded just above building level. Approximately 13 people were injured by flying glass.

Damaged tank on road, with burning oil fire,
during Operation Desert Storm

Monday, January 28, 1991

AS THE HOURS AND DAYS MOVED ALONG at a snail's pace, I entered a few details in my diary and my letters to the family back in Canada. Here's a sample.

On the evening of January 25, the impact shock of the missile imploded a wing of the Ministry of the Interior's registration building, officially causing 30 injuries and one death.

On January 26, a third Scud penetrated the Patriot defence system and struck near the Riyadh Airbase. The Scud fuselage may have received a glancing blow from a Patriot, but the warhead exploded at ground level, creating a loud noise and plume of smoke that drifted over the southern half of the city.

And more from the diary:

PAT FREEMAN (WIFE OF THE U.S. AMBASSADOR) had a dozen or so women over to the American residence for coffee this morning. It was a good idea to get together for a chat. I had a nice time sitting beside a Malaysian woman whose husband is economic counsellor at the U.S. embassy. I'd like her to meet Mary Hutchings when Mary comes back. This woman had heard of Mary through Mary McKinnon (a Canadian) when the Hutchingses were posted in Korea.

The Americans stayed up till 6 this morning to watch the Buffalo Bills and the New York Giants compete for the Super Bowl in Tampa — apparently it was broadcast over much of the world for the first time because of the Gulf War. The contest went down to the wire: when the Bills just missed a last-minute field goal, the Giants won, 20—19!

Pat told me that a bomb was defused in the garden of the American ambassador to Indonesia yesterday. Also, the tennis court of his counterpart in Kampala was blown up shortly after he had finished a game. Whew!

Temperature at noon today was 9 degrees Celsius. Unusually cold.

Coalition forces have just become aware of a massive oil-spill in the Persian Gulf off the coast of Kuwait. The region will be affected for decades to come. It is being called the worst environmental catastrophe in the history of the world.

News from Israel tells how people are apprehensive of biological weapons. Gawd!

Nolene Dabbagh was telling me this morning how difficult it was for Saudis to secure gas masks because members of the royal family had appropriated most of them and were selling them for profit. She denounced it as flagrant corruption, which is surprising even for the princes (as we know and love them). Her husband, Abdullah, was able to obtain a mask only recently, many days after they were supposed to be available.

Tuesday, January 29, 1991

COCKINGS HAD LENNART ALVIN (SWEDEN) and us over for dinner last night. It really was a pleasure to escape the Diplomatic Quarter and enjoy an evening free of worry. As it turned out, however, a missile arrived while we were having dinner. I had told Atta to be sure to come in if he heard an alarm, so, sure enough, the doorbell rang and Atta was there to tell us of the attack. The Cockings' maid becomes quite upset when the siren sounds; she was pleased to discover that Atta is Eritrean too, and was able to calm down somewhat. Subsequent reports tell us that four Patriot missiles were fired in defence, and the Scud was intercepted. No sign of chemicals or bacteria.

Celina Cocking has been with her parents since early November because of her mononucleosis. She and Anna are going to spend a week in Jeddah as the finale of her 'holiday,' and then she will go on to London. Anna is thinking of going to London too because Nick will be up north (in Saudi Arabia) with the National Guard for a couple of weeks.

Canadian Hercules planes are bringing equipment for the Canadian field hospital to be set up near the front, at Al-Qaysumah. Ottawa has offered to send the empty aircraft to Riyadh to pick up Canadians today, but Allan has told them no need: an American plane leaving today with 20 spaces for Canadians has only six takers. The Saudi government processes exit visas at a stately pace. I think about 90 Canadians are beginning now to prepare to leave Riyadh.

Royal Canadian Air Force C-130 Hercules, a four-engine turbine military aircraft in service since the 1950s

CHAPTER 16

Scuds, Scalpels, *and* Escapes
(February 1991)

Saturday, February 2, 1991

W E WERE SO PLEASED TO RECEIVE a faxed letter from John. Sorry he had to phone to let us know the machine wasn't working. It was great to hear that Abby is doing a lot of skiing. That will be a sport she will enjoy all her life.

Allan is having the ambassadors of Britain, Australia, and New Zealand over for a working lunch today. Tomorrow evening, about eight men for dinner to say good-bye to Colonel Clark Little. Activities seem virtually normal.

Jennifer Galpin delivered a baby girl last night at 11:45. Her name is Kristianne Jasmine Clark Galpin and she weighed 8 pounds. This morning Atta took over flowers and a note from us. Albert will take a few days off when Jennifer and the baby come home from the hospital. Then they will decide if it is necessary for them to go to Jeddah or Canada or not.

Atta has a problem with his eye and is to have laser surgery on it this afternoon. He doesn't expect to have to stay in the hospital. Allan made sure that Atta's brother Yassin would be free to drive him. Atta's family has been in Jeddah since the weekend before the war began. Schools are still on their spring break, which has been extended to February 16.

Sunday, February 3, 1991

OUR GOOD FRIEND THE PATRIOT MISSILE intercepted a Scud last night around 12:45 a.m. Radio reports two homes badly damaged and others with broken windows, etc., but apparently because of falling debris, not an explosion.

Last night we watched Peter Jennings's show on NBC answering children's questions about the war. It was a good approach. I hope our grandchildren had a chance to watch it. If not, perhaps NBC will show it again. The youngsters expressed the dilemma we all feel. We don't like war because we don't want people to be injured or killed. But the Iraqi dictator, with his chemical, biological, and nuclear potential, as well as his huge army and masses of military equipment, has conquered one country and threatens others in the region, including Saudi Arabia and Israel.

Wednesday, February 6, 1991

WE WENT TO THE EASTERN PROVINCE on Monday the 4th, leaving right after lunch. Military attaché Colonel Mel McLeod went with us, and Master Sergeant Ray drove to provide security (his machine-gun beside him).

We arrived in Dammam in time for a briefing by Andrew

Shisko and Corporal Alain LeClerc, before going for dinner with Canadian wardens at a restaurant. Andrew and Alain have been superb at keeping in touch with the Canadians in the Eastern Province. They've needed lots of tact and diplomacy to calm people when they became very agitated and strangely dependent on the government. I told Andrew it astonished me that Canadians seemed so keen to have the government decide what they should do, and when and how to leave, and I wondered why. He replied: they had worked for a long time for Aramco, which pays for almost everything — housing, holidays, schooling for children — and generally looks after their interests. Now, for life-and-death decisions, they insist that the Canadian government take care of them.

Issuing gas masks at the beginning of the war had helped calm them. Then, later, arranging for a 'voluntary departure' on American flights relieved the pressure on Andrew enormously. There is still another level of tension to expect, however. Allan believes that when the Iraqis deploy chemical weapons, there will be a massive call on the embassy to do something for the Canadians who still remain.

Believe it or not, among the 475 Canadians in the Eastern Province now, 90 are children! Why on earth would those families stay? Some have no place to go — undoubtedly, some are Lebanese or Palestinian Canadians. But, according to Andrew, some even have homes in Canada where they could go.

We had a Chinese dinner with Roy and Cathy Gunther-Smith, Norma and her husband, the doctor from Oakville, David Spicer, who works with the Saudi Electric Company (SECO), and another couple whose name I didn't hear. Allan would like to arrange for a letter from Joe Clark to all the wardens when the war is over. They are a very cooperative and helpful lot. Certainly the embassy wouldn't be able to do its consular work these days without them.

We left for Jubail about 8:30 p.m. We were pleased to have Alain lead the way in his car, because finding the way out of Dammam was really tricky, with detours and roadblocks along the way. We stayed at the Holiday Inn in Jubail, and had a good night's sleep.

The next morning Andrew met Allan and Mel at 8. They had a breakfast meeting with Commander Margaret Kavanagh, head of the administration for the medical end of things in the Gulf. She is a naval doctor stationed in Bahrain and reports to Commodore Summers. Also meeting them was Colonel Dr Claude Auger, who is chief of surgery at the Canadian Forces Hospital in Halifax. He is leading Canada's medical Operation Scalpel for the war and is acting commanding officer of the temporary Jubail command centre receiving equipment for the hospital they are building at Al-Qaysumah, just behind the front line.

While we chatted with the military personnel, waiting for Ca-

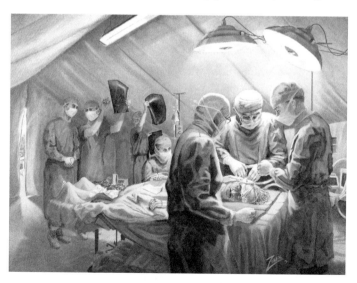

Al Qaysumah, First Canadian Field Hospital, Saudi Arabia, by Edward Zuber, Operation Friction, Persian Gulf, 1991

nadian journalists, Colonel Auger showed us an operating room set up in a tent. This week, military experts were lecturing doctors on treating cases at the front. These 60 or so doctors will go up to Al-Qaysumah at week's end, and others are flying from Canada for similar instruction and assignment. A ship is bringing

A sketch of Colonel Dr Claude Auger at Al-Qaysumah by Edward Zuber

more personnel and equipment, so Al-Qaysumah will have 500 medics by early March.

We moved on, driving for several hours to the field hospital at Al-Qaysumah, and found ourselves stepping high through mud and construction materials and soldiers unpacking medical equipment for installation in new wooden buildings.

I had a good conversation there with three women — Commander Kavanagh; a major who is a doctor; and a captain who is in charge of logistics. The captain's family now lives in North Bay, Ontario, and she had recently become engaged to a soldier who is also responsible for logistics. He is stationed in Bahrain, so they see each other occasionally. They both came from Petawawa, Ontario. She said her parents are pretty concerned, but her father has come to grips with her being near the front. She was hoping that wedding plans would provide a healthy distraction for her mother.

Another doctor showed me the T-shirts that have been designed for their unit. They're great — a beaver on a red circular background, with some medical insignia, and "Dusty Beaver" written in English, French, and Arabic. I'd love to be able to get three of them.

Back in Jubail later that day Allan, Mel, and Andrew called

on our friend Prince Abdullah, of the Royal Commission, who spoke about his various concerns about the situation in Kuwait and, when Allan pressed him, welcomed any assistance with the Gulf oil-spill. (The wardens we dined with the previous night were ready to help with the cleanup.)

Our drive home took about four hours, and we arrived before 9 o'clock. Master Sergeant Ray did a fine job, keeping a sharp eye on Allan the whole time. He told us that his boss (Luke) had told him he couldn't leave Allan's side for any reason. I guess I was lucky he hadn't been sleeping on our couch during the night.

We enjoyed getting to know Mel McLeod and becoming more familiar with the mandate of a defence attaché. He is very diplomatic, and very careful not to tread on anyone's toes. He will meet Commodore Summers and wants to have a good, cooperative relationship with him, while maintaining a distance, so that Summers doesn't think he has a call on him. His mission is diplomacy and intelligence, so he'll get to know people in the Saudi Ministry of Defence, National Guard, etc. Allan is having a luncheon next Tuesday to introduce him to the military attachés of the NATO countries.

Wednesday, February 13, 1991

WE HAVE RECEIVED MAIL BY BAG (diplomatic pouch) and by the regular mail system. Letters from each of the kids were written about January 15, and they all sound very concerned about us. I am so glad to have these messages from them.

Ginny Sincock sent over a sample T-shirt entitled "Scudbusters." It has a picture of a camel and palm trees, with a Scud missile being intercepted by a Patriot above. On the back is "Saudi Arabia,

January 1991." The shirts are available only in a large size and sell for 50 riyals, plus any donation for a fund for the armed forces. I asked Ginny to save a half-dozen for me. Meanwhile, I'll take the sample to the embassy to see if anyone else wants to buy some. I'm sure it will be very popular.

Allan had the NATO defence attachés for lunch yesterday. He said they all seemed to appreciate it. They meet every morning at 11 a.m. and invited Colonel Mel McLeod to join them from now on.

We are having Nolene and Abdullah Dabbagh for dinner tonight. Also the Mehtas, Paul Moreau, and Fahd Somait, to make a nice little group of eight. Should be pleasant. The Dabbaghs have lent us a bunch of videos again. We particularly enjoyed the Hallmark playhouse feature called *The Shellseekers*. I told David when he called from Houston that Allan and I were both shedding sentimental tears over the Hallmark ad about Christmas with the family!

Larry Dickenson is coming from Bahrain for a couple of days. He'll arrive Friday afternoon. Since that is the weekend and we don't want to overwork the A-team unnecessarily, I suggested that Hanif leave a casserole and salad for us, and we'll look after ourselves for dinner Friday night. Tough, eh?

Saturday, three officials from External Affairs are arriving for meetings about post-war issues. We'll have them for dinner Saturday night and lunch on Sunday before they leave. Sunday night we are having six or seven people in for dinner with Larry. Alex McGoldrick (Australia) knows him well because Alex is accredited to Kuwait and the other Gulf countries too, and Larry has been quite helpful to him because he has been on the spot.

Allan is doing a TV interview for the Saudi Channel One this morning. He is also trying to arrange a phone call between Prince Saud al Faisal (Saudi foreign minister) and Joe Clark (our minister of external affairs).

You should see the set-up our immigration and visa guys have at the embassy, as I wrote to the kids. Because of security measures, only a certain few people may enter the embassy. To facilitate screening and processing, Dave Clark and Greg have set up a table outside, close to the guardhouse inside the gate. They have an umbrella over the table, and a sign that says, "SCUD Café"! I must get a picture of it. And in short order we will surely rename our staff room (the Wadi Club) the 'SCUD Café'!

The Wadi Club becomes the SCUD Café.

Speaking of pictures, when we had a farewell dinner for Colonel Clark Little, who has gone back to Canada to take command of the military installation at North Bay, Clark gave Allan two blown-up pictures he had taken of the gang at the Wadi Club: before and after — one of the gang as they appear normally, the other of the same group wearing their gas masks. A keepsake. Some day we'll chuckle. (But we will never hear the wailing sounds of sirens again without shuddering.)

The Wadi Club with no gas masks

Saturday, February 23, 1991

WE SEEM TO BE BUSY. It sounds like a merry round of social activities, but we exchange a lot of information and make plans during these very enjoyable events. Thursday evening we had dinner at Al Rashids'. Spain and India were there too. It was a lovely evening, with Mouna Al Rashid as exhilarating as ever.

Friday the Laceys held a lunch in their garden (he's head of Bechtel in the Middle East). It was fun to talk to vigorous, personable Bechtel people from the United States. They are preparing to help reconstruct Kuwait, as well as cleaning up the Gulf oil-spill.

Monday I am invited to Harriet Buschman's for coffee. She had a baby boy. I had assumed she had left the Kingdom, so was surprised to hear from her. Meanwhile, Allan is having in for lunch an official from Ottawa responsible for immigration operations.

Tuesday, I am off to visit the nursery school of the Indian embassy with the ambassador's wife. Following that, I will be heading to a bridge luncheon to say farewell to Beth, whose military husband is retiring at the end of the month. That evening Allan and I will be dropping in at a Turkish reception to say good-bye to Ambassador Namek, who represents the United Nations Development Programme (UNDP) here. Wednesday, another bridge game.

All of this is very pleasant, and it still leaves me the evenings to spend with Allan, although actually we just received an invitation to go for dinner at the Italian residence, so maybe the old social life is beginning to pick up. Perhaps the major difference these days is that there are so few of our Saudi friends here in Riyadh. Teymour and Faisa Alireza are in England. Teymour has been doing public-relations work for the Saudi government in Japan, while Faisa and the children have stayed in their home in London.

While all this goes on, it seems that there will be a dreadful increase in war activity. It really is horrible to think of the injuries and deaths that will result from the continuing war. What a shame that Saddam Hussein doesn't face what we think is inevitable and withdraw. Also, I would have thought that there might be some way to accomplish it using Moscow's attempts to mediate.

U.S. tanks and artillery advance across desert
in southern Iraq during ground war, February 1991.

February 24, 1991

THE LAND WAR BEGAN TODAY. In the wee hours, the coalition's forces invaded Kuwait and Iraq. As I was saying to Allan at lunchtime, the weird thing about this war is that we see no pictures of people being carried on stretchers. The aerial bombardment by the coalition forces has meant few casualties and deaths among 'our' forces. And we have seen no evidence of even those few. We hear from military briefings that our forces have 'killed' a certain number of tanks or knocked out so many bridges. Airplanes have made a hundred thousand (!!!) sorties during the month of war. We can't imagine the damage they have done. And we have no notion of the suffering of people in Iraq. We are beginning to read stories in the press about torture and murder of Kuwaitis. All of this is awful. But somehow one feels numb. We wait for it to be over so we can finally go on holidays. How strange to be so unfeeling.

Fighting has taken place on the Saudi—Iraqi border, with 40 Iraqi troops killed near Al Khafgi. The United States has offered to provide military flights out of the Eastern Province for Americans wishing to leave — the first assistance it has provided. It has not offered gas masks or issued advisories to dependants to leave, as we have.

The United States is sending Israel more Patriot anti-missile missiles. British Prime Minister John Major has said that the Iraqis still have a substantial, unknown number of mobile Scud missile launchers. A press announcement in Riyadh discloses that Iraqi prisoners were captured in Kuwait.

Allan is run off his feet. Even so, he sent a note to the staff.

This is a time when everyone associated with our embassy here in Riyadh is operating under unusual stress. I want you to know that your professional response to the current strains is enormously appreciated by Canadians in the

Kingdom, the Department of External Affairs in Ottawa, and by me.

We look at the courage and dedication of personnel like Andrew Shisko and Alain LeClerc who are providing leadership and support to the Canadian community in the Eastern Province. We appreciate the way Wayne House responded to the request to set up the office in Al Khobar. Wives and children have taken necessary decisions and, without complaint, are spending anxious time away from their husbands and fathers. They deserve medals.

The rest of you in Riyadh are doing a magnificent job! Donald McLennan is distributing the masks in record time. Our contingency plans are in excellent shape thanks to Ron Bollman and the work of the Emergency Task Force, which is meeting daily now. Our wardens are fully informed by Albert Galpin and his able assistants. David Hutchings, Norma Shearer and Pam Saunders have been working non-stop to ensure effective communication between Ottawa and the Gulf, and that means that Charles Hall has had heavy loads of work. Klaus has effectively headed the administration of such a busy and growing embassy with the able assistance of Colin Suter. Dave Clark seems like one of the 'family' since he has pitched in to cover immigration responsibilities formerly handled in Kuwait. And how glad we are to have the excellent group of military personnel with us during this crisis. Indeed everyone at the embassy — Canada-based and locally engaged alike — has pitched in to meet the challenges.

ON FEBRUARY 28, THE LIBERATION OF KUWAIT WAS COMPLETE — the war was, in effect, over.

PART SIX

A Semblance *of* Normality
(March 1991—New Year 1992)

CHAPTER 17

MOVERS *and* SHAKERS

Saturday, March 9, 1991

IT'S BEEN A LONG TIME since I made an entry in this diary. I was exhausted by the war and drained of anything more to write. Only now do I feel like beginning to keep track of what is going on again. Even now I am making an entry only because so much is happening that I really don't want to lose it.

Last Sunday I wrote to Allan's cousins Neil and Ruth:

We are so relieved that the war is over, and with so few casualties on the side of the 'good guys.' As time goes on and we discover how many Iraqis have been wounded and killed we'll feel very badly about the consequences of war, but I must admit that at this moment it is just an enormous relief to have it ended. (Let's hope the ceasefire sticks.)

Allan is very tired and is looking forward to seeing all the family. This week, however, he is arranging a visit by Joe Clark and a group of businessmen to talk with Saudi and Kuwaiti officials about reconstruction. Bill McKnight (our Minister of Defence) is also arriving this week to visit the troops and congratulate them on a job well done. So Allan and his people at the embassy will continue to work under pressure. The household staff, too, has to prepare dinners and receptions for the visitors. Hopefully all will be quiet enough in a couple of weeks for everybody to catch up on rest and recreation! Then for us it's off to Canada!

Allan has been busy trying to arrange the Clark visit ever since then. He couldn't pin the Saudis down to a program no matter how hard he tried. He worked through Madani, then Mansouri, Kurdi, and other senior Saudi officials. Eventually they admitted that they had ten other foreign ministers visiting at the time Clark wanted to come (the GCC six plus Egypt, Italy, Syria, and the United States). Poor Saudis.

But Clark was already on his way to Israel, Syria, Jordan, etc. Allan flew to Taif in the west at four in the morning — after a big dinner party here, which had been previously arranged to say farewell to the Australian ambassador — to meet Mr Clark and his delegation and to discuss the major obstacles to an official visit. Allan suggested a 'working' visit, and Clark agreed to send a personal letter to Prince Saud, who was attending the security meeting of foreign ministers in Damascus. It worked.

So, at a moment's notice, the visit was on. In the meantime, we were already welcoming arrivals of the 21 Canadian businessmen who had been invited to accompany Mr Clark. We had Don Matthews, president of Matthews Construction, and former ambassador to Iran Ken Taylor, who was now acting as consultant to Matthews Construction, for dinner Wednesday night. With them, too, was a close friend of Prime Minister Mulroney's, Sam Wakim (a lawyer with Fasken & Calvin law firm in Toronto). Apparently the prime minister wants us to pay special attention to Matthews (although Clark does not!). Then, next day, we had five people from Canadian Helicopters, led by Craig Dobbin, for lunch. They gave us a beautiful sculpture by Newfoundlander Nathaniel Noel.

But two ministerial visits at once! Right after lunch we left by car for Jubail, where Allan met Defence Minister McKnight early the next morning so they could visit the Canadian field hospital at Al-Qaysumah. We left there about noon, with lunch in the car, so that Allan could swing into action as soon as he got home.

He had time only for a quick shower, then went off to the Intercontinental Hotel to welcome officially the businessmen in Joe Clark's delegation and to brief them formally. They all went to Teymour and Faisa Alirezas' for a reception (which hospitality Allan appreciated very much).

Allan left Teymour's home to meet the incoming Joe Clark at the military airport. Meanwhile the businessmen came here to the embassy. Finally everyone gathered for a really successful buffet dinner for 36 people. It was Clark's first opportunity to meet the delegation and to speak to them formally.

Allan and the minister were pleased to meet Prince Saud Al Faisal, who invited them to his palace for an informal dinner tonight, which would include the Italian foreign minister, U.S. Secretary of State James Baker, and their ambassadors *and wives*.

Monday, March 11, 1991 (AND WIVES TOO!)

"WOMEN AND MEN TOGETHER in the same reception?!" I was astonished to hear of the invitation. The dinner at Prince Saud's palace was very likely the first time our host and his wife, Princess Johara, had entertained women and men together. I had been at the palace before, but only with a lot of ambassadors' wives and various female members of the royal family.

I was to be at the palace at 9 p.m., and Allan and the minister at 9:30. This worked out very well, because the men didn't have to rush away from the reception at the residence. In fact, Clark was able to lie down for a few minutes.

When I arrived at the palace, Prince Saud's brother, Prince Turki, head of Saudi intelligence, was on hand to greet guests, along with Saud's wife, Princess Johara. Also present were the wives of Minister of Petroleum Hasham Nazzer, intelligence chief Prince Turki, and the minister of finance. Female guests were Vivi Maolini (Italy) and Pat Freeman (U.S.) with Susan Baker, Jim's wife.

Eventually the men arrived and, surprisingly, joined the women. It was clear that Princess Johara was pretty uncomfortable with this mixed group, but Prince Saud was masterful at moving people around and encouraging them to mix. The group included General Schwarzkopf, James Baker, Foreign Minister Gianni De Michelis of Italy, the foreign ministers of Canada, Egypt, and Syria, the Saudi ministers of petroleum and finance, Italian Ambassador Mario Maolini, U.S. Ambassador Chas Freeman, the ambassadors of Egypt and Syria, and Allan.

What a treat! It really was riveting to be part of a small group like that, so prominent among the people who are debating peace and security for the Middle East for years to come. And what a charming lot they were. General Schwarzkopf, by the way, is a very personable man, whose face lights up with goodwill as he chats about all the phases of the recent campaign and his planning for them. He says he is keen to return home to his wife and three children — 20, 19, and 13. But he is concerned that the cease-fire has not yet been signed.

I had a nice chat before dinner with Egyptian Foreign Minister Amr Moussa. He told me that he had been ambassador to the United Nations 12 years earlier, when Egypt signed the peace treaty with Israel, which was so unpopular with the rest of the Arab countries. (In fact, as I recall, Egypt was kicked out of the Arab League because of it.) He said he was certainly persona non grata among the Arab representatives at the UN then.

But now he is very pleased that Egypt took such a strong and consistent stand against Iraq right from the start and can now take a lead diplomatically. In response to my probing, he also expressed concern about the eventual regime in Iraq. The Shiites are strong contenders and would be very much influenced by their co-religionists in Iran. Iranians, in his view, are still not to be trusted. Amr Moussa was a fascinating man to talk to.

At a dinner table for eight, I sat between Joe Clark and General Schwarzkopf. Also at our table was the Syrian foreign minister, who kept asking the general if it would not be a good idea

General Norman Schwarzkopf leads Desert Storm
Victory Parade, Washington, DC, June 8, 1991.

to go into Iraq and finish off Saddam's regime, since he was clearly committing atrocities against his own people. The general replied that that was not in the UN mandate. But it was interesting to realize that Syria wouldn't mind seeing the war continue. As a matter of fact, some time during the evening I heard mention that the Iraqi regime is using chemicals against the opposition. I hope no one is trying to use that as an excuse to go back to war.

General Schwarzkopf said that he believed that Saddam had no more chemical capability. Apparently the shelf life is only six weeks. The plants were bombed at the beginning of the air war. The general believed that the Iraqis did use chemicals with their artillery during the ground war, but to no effect, because they had dissipated. He seemed firmly convinced that the signed agreement had to end the war; otherwise the coalition of allied nations would have collapsed.

Joe Clark was very nice about telling various people that I was the first woman officer of the House of Commons.

Halfway through the meal, Prince Saud took him and Allan away to call on the Custodian of the Two Holy Mosques. Later the Italian foreign minister and ambassador departed for the same reason. So I went home after the party about 12:30 a.m., and Allan arrived home about 1:30.

Next morning he saw Joe Clark and his party off to Kuwait, went to a luncheon for James Baker, then drove with Atta to Dhahran, where Minister McKnight was guest of honour at a large dinner for the Canadian businessmen hosted by a Saudi. This morning, Allan came back to Riyadh and brought with him Hugh Mullington, president of the Ottawa-based Canadian Commercial Corporation, to stay overnight before he goes on to Harare, Zimbabwe.

Hugh is a very nice person who has stayed with us before. He brought Canadian newspapers and Laura Secord chocolates for us. It's always a pleasure to see him. Both Allan and Hugh are looking very tired. I told them I want them to have a good sleep before I meet them at dinnertime. Meanwhile, I'm going to an art exhibition at the American residence.

Kuwaitis celebrate on the streets of Kuwait City following their liberation by coalition forces, March 1991.

Abby Goes *to* Paris

April 1991

IN APRIL 1991, WITH THE WAR OVER, we had a wonderful holiday in Canada with our family and then departed — with grand-daughter Abby — for France! The evening before, we had all gone out to dinner to a new restaurant, North 44 on Yonge Street, north of Eglinton. It was really good. Brenda accompanied John. It was Allan's first opportunity to meet her. I had had lunch earlier in the week with John, Brenda, Jill, and David. It was a lovely last evening. We had been visiting with all our children so much over the previous three weeks that I thought they must surely have tired of us. But if they had, they hid it well. Our whole time in Canada was a treasure of family togetherness. My goodness, I love those kids!

So Abby Hazlewood Lever, daughter of John Hazlewood Lever, went with us to France! What a treat for Allan and me to spend the week with her. And she was wonderful company. I had expected a certain normal amount of whining or objecting to what I suggested for clothes and activities. But she was a perfect travelling companion.

We flew all night to Paris. Abby had a book with her and enjoyed it along with dinner and a Belushi movie. In fact, I don't think she slept more than 15 minutes. We changed planes at Charles de Gaulle airport and made our way to Nice. There Mouna Al Rashid's driver, Grégoire, met us and took us to the Hotel Negresco.

That evening we had dinner with Mouna and a half-dozen other guests aboard her new yacht in the harbour of Monaco. Abby was marvellous at coping with the long meal, which lasted through several courses. We had a tour of the boat — seven decks high, 310 feet long. It is pretty swell! Abby enjoyed the children's playroom with pinball machines and many other games.

Next day we returned to Monaco to visit the aquaria at the Oceanographic Museum, which Jacques Cousteau ran for years. We also saw the changing of the guard at the Prince's Palace, home to the ruling Grimaldis for over 700 years, and currently to the widowed Prince Rainier.

Sunday was a day we spent in Nice. We enjoyed some time at the beach in front of the hotel, but the highlight was our visit to the Musée Marc Chagall. Wonderful building for housing the master's very colourful paintings and stained-glass windows. We also visited the flower market in the old part of town, which was within walking distance of our hotel. Favourite spot for lunch

Allan and Abby in Paris

was McDonald's, and we enjoyed La Rotonde in the hotel for dinner. Abby coped wonderfully well with the time change. She stayed up quite late with us, then slept till after 9 in the morning. We enjoyed our breakfasts served in the room.

Monday provided an outing into the countryside near Nice. We visited St-Paul de Vence, where we thoroughly enjoyed la Fondation Maeght — a magnificent gallery of modern art that hugs a spectacular treed location overlooking the town. Sculptures by Miró and Giacometti adorn the gardens as well as the gallery itself. Abby bought a couple of postcards with pictures of the works she enjoyed the most.

We went on up to Tourrettes-sur-Loup, a charming little village that friends had recommended. Lunch there was delightful. Then we dashed back to the Mediterranean to Antibes, in time to catch the show of whales and dolphins at the aquarium there. (Abby was big on 'aquaria.') While in Antibes we also visited the Musée Picasso, located in a charming old house — formerly the

Musée Picasso in Antibes

Château Grimaldi — where the artist had lived by the sea. Allan enjoyed looking at all the sailboats tied up there too.

Tuesday we flew to Paris. This was to be a short stay. We had only one full day there, so did as much as we could in the time available. In the morning, Abby and I took a bus ride through the city. I had hoped the commentary would be entirely in French, but unfortunately there were earphones with several languages available. It was really much easier for both Abby and me to understand the English, so finally we both gave in.

Allan took Abby to the Eiffel Tower in the afternoon while I sampled the French impressionists in the Musée d'Orsay. Later we wandered through Notre Dame and made our way to the Louvre. Allan and I were both surprised at Abby's interest in the art in the Louvre as we searched for the *Mona Lisa*. There was a room full of Rubenses, and many medieval paintings that she stopped to admire.

We dined at the Canadian ambassador's official residence in the rue du Faubourg Saint-Honoré, near the Champs Elysées. It was great to see Claude and Marguerite Charland after a couple of years. Their home is lovely. Allan had seen it before, of course, but I had not. I would have liked a tour of the whole place, but we spent the evening in the Charlands' private quarters.

Off to London the next day. We stayed at the Hyde Park Residences on Park Lane and had a flat that was just perfect — attractively decorated, lots of space, and kitchen equipped with microwave, dishwasher, and even washer and dryer.

With Abby we saw *Miss Saigon*. The music and story were good, but I just hope the scenes in bawdy houses didn't adversely affect Abby.

Abby left on Air Canada on Saturday morning and, according to John, had a fine trip home, enjoying the meal, movie, and a nice woman who sat beside her.

During the rest of our holiday, we went to Jean Anouilh's play *The*

Rehearsal and Yehudi Menuhin's 75th-birthday concert, where he played a Bach concerto for violins with his 16-year-old student. He also conducted the London Philharmonic Orchestra and the Royal Choral Singers in Beethoven's 9th Symphony. Great performances. Other evenings we entertained. We had Belle Shenkman and Desmond Smith for drinks at the flat, followed by dinner at Allan's favourite restaurant, Le Caprice, in St James's. We did the same thing a couple of nights later with Joanna Cocking and her husband, Martin, and Celina Cocking and her boyfriend, William. In the apartment hotel we could entertain as well as cook our own meals. Possibly a saving overall, even though the flat itself was almost as expensive as a room in the Sheraton Park Tower.

We travelled back to Riyadh via Switzerland for a change. When Teymour Alireza heard that we planned to stay in Zurich for a couple of nights, he insisted we come on to Geneva instead and stay with them. I wasn't too keen on the idea — being an anti-social sort of gal — but we did do that. It was wonderful! Their home is set on a hill looking north across Lake Geneva towards the mountains. The weather was beautiful, and the view was the most breathtaking panorama I have ever seen — a delight.

I had been in Geneva only once before: for one rainy, cold day in March. My mental picture of the city and its environs was black and white, but now it has changed completely. It must surely be the most beautiful place in the world.

Friday, May 3, 1991

HOME AGAIN IN RIYADH, our main focus has been the 40 or so Canadian businessmen led by new Minister of Industry, Science, Technology and International Trade Michael Wilson. The A-team coped superbly with a luncheon on Friday and a buffet dinner for 60 that evening. Next day I gave a ladies' luncheon for Margie Wilson, and in the evening we had a reception for about 200 in the garden. It was particularly successful: people spread out on the lawn so that it didn't seem too crowded at any one spot. We had installed a couple of spotlights on the roof to shine down gently on the garden, and we also had purchased a dozen or so additional brass candle-holders and lanterns to create a pleasant glow.

There was a concert in the atrium the same night as the reception. We were sorry to miss it and worried a bit about the large crowd coming all on one night, but it worked out all right. People seem to appreciate our willingness to host the concerts, so goodwill abounds.

On Sunday the mission went to Jeddah for meetings and for the minister to address a Chamber of Commerce luncheon. Margie Wilson and I had a delightful day there with Nadia Zahid,

Allan with the Honourable Michael Wilson

wife of Sheikh Talal, our honorary consul-general. We visited a jewellery shop, where we saw some pieces designed by Nadia, then on to an antique shop. Margie Wilson bought a Persian rug and was quite pleased. After a quick lunch, we dashed back to the airport for our return to Riyadh with all the others. (We were in a chartered Saudia plane.)

Since the mission left, we have been busy. Everyone seems to be celebrating the fact that the war is over and friends have returned. Also, this is the season to say 'farewell' to people who are leaving for other posts. The Austrian ambassador is leaving on Monday; in their honour we went to a luncheon on a Saudi farm last Thursday and will go to dinners tonight and tomorrow. The Mehtas are posted for four months in New York before going to Hong Kong, where he will be general manager of the Hongkong and Shanghai Banking Corporation (HSBC). The Van Eses had a dinner for them last week, and I am going to several lunches for Aruna in the next couple of weeks.

It's probably exceptionally busy now, too, because it's the short period between the two great Muslim holidays: Eid al-Fitr ('festival of breaking of the fast,' after the last day of Ramadan: April 15 in 1991), and Eid al-Adha ('festival of the sacrifice,' the feast of the hajj, beginning 18 June in 1991). After the hajj, most people will be away for summer holidays.

Yemen will be celebrating the first anniversary of unification on May 22. Allan will have to go to Sana'a for that, but I don't expect to.

I am reading avidly about the game of bridge these days, so as not to be totally humiliated by my stupidity at the bridge table. There is a group of women who play regularly and have been including me in their games for the last few months. Unfortunately for me, they are much more expert than I am.

I have also been doing some required reading in preparation

for the teaching course I'm going to take in London in June. Fun.

Allan met Prince Salman, governor of Riyadh, this morning to invite him formally for an official trip to Canada as the guest of Senator Guy Charbonneau, Speaker of the upper house. This is for the Canadian opening of the exhibition "Kingdom Yesterday and Today," which the Custodian of the Two Holy Mosques had so kindly agreed to send, in response to Allan's request when he presented his credentials. The visitors will arrive in Canada on July 10.

Tuesday, August 13, 1991

AS A GESTURE OF HOSPITALITY AND FRIENDSHIP, Senator Charbonneau invited Prince Salman and his delegation to a dinner at the Ritz Hotel in Montreal. Word came to Allan from the Saudi ambassador that no wine could be served.

"Speaker Charbonneau has invited his friends and other men he holds in high regard," Allan told me.

"This won't do!" he sputtered. "I know he prides himself on his knowledge and appreciation of fine wines. He would be so disappointed."

So Allan spoke directly to Prince Salman about the matter. His reply was reassuring. "No problem. Certainly wine can be served. Our Saudi people just won't have any." In the event, delicious wines were presented to guests after the press had taken their pictures and departed.

The exhibition was well received, and we cherish from that time a picture of Allan and the mayor of Riyadh, along with accompanying dignitaries, sitting side by side, Saudi-style, on a Persian rug. It is framed in gold, of course.

Then, in January, responding to Prince Salman's invitation,

Speaker Charbonneau entertains Prince Salman
in Montreal, July 1991.

Allan and visitors sit side by side, Saudi style, during
Prince Salman's visit, with his 60-member entourage, to
Montreal to open "The Kingdom Yesterday and Today" in July 1991.

Speaker Charbonneau came to Riyadh with his wife, Yolande. Prince Salman expected the couple to stay at the royal guest palace, but the Speaker indicated to Allan that they would much prefer to stay with us. We were delighted to have them.

They did the rounds of sightseeing and receptions, and Allan took them on a trip to Yemen as well. While with us, they kindly presented us with the huge 1986 volume entitled *Canada: From Sea unto Sea*, inscribing inside the cover, "To Nora and Allan, with our very warm wishes and thanks for your charming hospitality, Yolande & Guy Charbonneau."

Sunday, August 25, 1991

RETURNING FROM OUR VACATION last Tuesday evening, Allan went to the office on Wednesday; then had a nice, leisurely weekend Thursday and Friday to catch up on the files. We've both enjoyed our morning swims again. It's a great routine. Skies are bright blue and sunny, as we remembered them, and everything about the place is a delight to come home to.

The A-team had had a good holiday in Pakistan. Ali and Hanif showed me pictures of their two families together. Hanif (and Zafar) live close to or in the city of Rawalpindi, which is almost part of Islamabad. Ali's family has lived for generations up in the high hilly countryside about three hours away by car. The countryside around Ali's house is beautiful, with pine trees that look much like those in Canada. It is about 3,000 metres above sea level, lovely in the summer (with quite a bit of rain) and very cold in the winter. By contrast, Hanif said, the city is in the plain and is very hot right now.

They both have fine-looking families. Hanif has eight children, I believe, and Ali has five or six. A couple of Ali's children have married and there are grandchildren in the pictures too. The A-team, too, don't seem unhappy to be back in Riyadh. (It's a wonderful 'hardship' posting!)

All four of our children are planning to visit us for two weeks at Christmas. (Allan is able to convert some of his holiday time to family travel for 'family reunification.' We're hoping that will go a long way towards purchase of tickets.)

As I was putting photos in a new album I bought at the Al Akariyah souk this week, I came across some pictures of camels the grandchildren might like to see, but I won't mail them just yet because of the postal strike in Canada. (Thank goodness for fax machines.)

This afternoon we're having Pam Saunders and her husband, Colin Suter, along with their houseguests, Ian Burney and his spouse, in for a drink. They were posted in Thailand and are just on their way back to Ottawa for "three to five" (years), as they say in the foreign service.

I accepted an invitation for bridge tomorrow morning. Here we go again. (Whiling away one's time playing bridge symbolizes the epitome of utter decadence to me. It is, however, a nice way to see the gang whom I haven't seen since last spring.)

Wednesday, August 28, 1991

THIS MORNING WE MET with a group of people from the organization Friends of the Earth. They are concerned about the effect of Saddam's oil fires still burning in Kuwait on the environment all over this part of the world. It seems to be taking too long for the Kuwaiti government to cap the fires, and they are wondering if other countries and environmental associations ought to be helping.

CHAPTER 18

EMBASSY *and* CLASSROOM

TEFL Certificate

ONCE I HAD SETTLED into the rhythm of the diplomatic life in Riyadh, I began to wonder if I should be returning to 'work.' Some of the wives from other embassies were teaching in Saudi schools, and it seemed a terrific way to involve myself with the social milieu of this very unusual country.

"But I'm not qualified," said the little voice inside my head. I had taught piano and theory many years earlier, but found it frustrating, especially when I had my own small children scrambling over a student to play random notes on the piano.

Through the British Council Office in Riyadh I learned of a well-respected school in London, called International House. It was then at 106 Piccadilly, an 18th-century mansion, not far from the Canadian High Commission on Grosvenor Square. What possibilities lay there, I imagined. It offered a month-long course in teaching English as a foreign language. It might let me see if I enjoyed teaching as well as giving me the qualifications to do it.

Allan arranged for me to stay for the month in a tiny flat upstairs at the high commission. It worked wonderfully. Each morning I was able to walk to the school. Lunch breaks could be in Green Park across the street. And at 'home' in the high commission, I worked at all the assignments and various projects and preparations. Fun! Yes, I loved it!

In June 1991 the University of Cambridge Local Exam Syndicate (UCLES) awarded me its Certificate in Teaching English as a Foreign Language for Adults (CTEFLA).

Les jeunes françaises

MY FIRST JOB WAS TEACHING English at the French School for girls in Riyadh. I had known that the French system is somewhat rigid in its method and found it somewhat different from the fun and games at International House. But it was interesting to meet the students none the less.

One of these girls in my class for 13-year-olds wrote a great composition. "She's a real pill who misbehaves in class," I wrote in my diary. But she was very fond of riding. She wrote a 'letter' to her horse (a two-year-old being reared in some other country). She missed it very much, apparently. She even included a picture of it in her essay. She promised to

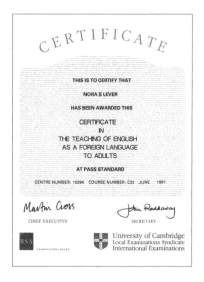

CERTIFICATE

THIS IS TO CERTIFY THAT

NORA S LEVER

HAS BEEN AWARDED THIS

CERTIFICATE
IN
THE TEACHING OF ENGLISH
AS A FOREIGN LANGUAGE
TO ADULTS

AT PASS STANDARD

CENTRE NUMBER: 10294 COURSE NUMBER: C32 JUNE 1991

Martin Cross
CHIEF EXECUTIVE

John Reddaway
SECRETARY

RSA
EXAMINATIONS BOARD

University of Cambridge
Local Examinations Syndicate
International Examinations

bring her album of pictures for me to see on Wednesday. (I hoped her behaviour in class would improve as she found her teacher to be really interested in what she cared about.)

Monday, August 26, 1991

I HAVE TALKED TO DR ILHAM, director of Riyadh's Institute of Public Administration regarding my teaching English. She seems to suggest some part-time classes available for me when the new term starts September 14. But she's being a bit vague about it. Is this the Saudi way of putting me off?

Yesterday I called on the director of the Language Centre for Girls, Mme Heba Afify. She says that their next term starts October 5, with registration the preceding week. She won't know until registration is complete whether she will need teachers. In the meantime she gave me the name of the texts they use.

I bought them at Al Jarir bookstore yesterday and find the material very good. The teacher's manual is exceptionally helpful, as it spells out how to approach each section of each lesson and uses methods very like those advanced at International House. The aim of the course is communication, and the functional approach is evident throughout. The second edition of the material, published in 1989, is colourful and provides a better teacher's guide than the 1980 edition.

Meanwhile I'm really keen to teach English. The schools won't be starting their programs for a few weeks, and registration will determine whether they will need me for a few hours each week. I'll keep my fingers crossed.

Sunday, September 1, 1991

WE'RE HAVING A SMALL GROUP for lunch today to say farewell to the departing ambassador of Bangladesh and his wife, whom I've enjoyed knowing over the last two years. There has been a change of government in Bangladesh, so General Dastgir is being 'retired.' We're having Indonesia, South Korea, Sri Lanka, and Thailand — all a good gang that we saw last night as well at the Malaysian National Day reception.

Tomorrow a lunch at the British residence honours the departing ambassador for Turkey. (It's the season, apparently, for departures.) Then there is a 5-o'clock tea for Nouran at the Danish embassy. Actually, I'm sorry to see her go. We played tennis a couple of times a week during the crisis last year.

Allan and I travelled to a campsite on the desert last Wednesday night. We were guests of the British military mission at the National Guard to say farewell to the Cockings. Some of the people stayed overnight. We did, along with the Cockings and Munros. So Allan served for breakfast a marvellous omelette (Hanif had chopped and packed the ingredients for us ahead of time). We had a couple of Kuwaiti rugs, table, folding chairs, single-burner stove, lanterns, etc. We also used a tablecloth, plates, cutlery, and all the fine things that the British seem to do when they go 'camping.' I said to Hanif when we were making lists in preparation that Canadians would sit on the ground when they were at a campsite. He observed that the British have had many years of experience in places like India, and their style of life hasn't been bad!

Next day we went 100 kilometres northwest to Thumamah Research Centre in King Khalid Wildlife Park, where a wildlife commission is pioneering in the rescue of almost-extinct species of animals. The property belonged to King Khalid until he died in 1982. Apparently he was very fond of wild animals and had imported some. So there were a few zebras and many ostriches. The main effort, however, is expanding the herds of gazelles. We were driven for about four hours over the desert and saw hundreds of them, such delicate, beautiful creatures. The ostriches are interesting, too. They stand over six feet tall and are spellbinding to see. Finally we saw a half-dozen very precious examples of the Arabian oryx; they, too, have been overhunted and are almost extinct. So the wildlife commission is doing great work.

When we got back home around 2 p.m. we were pretty weary and dehydrated. We had major naps and showers before going out for another farewell dinner at the Van Eses. We were pleased to be able to stay at home and veg yesterday.

Monday, September 9, 1991

I'M HIDING IN THE TV ROOM. Allan is having a reception in honour of the upcoming Joint Economic Commission meeting in Ottawa. The Canadian and Saudi foreign ministers, along with their officials and a business delegation, get together regularly to develop and expand trade opportunities.

Allan has invited about 150 Saudis and expects between sixty and a hundred. The reception is in the garden, and the full moon is enchanting! Ali has situated about 30 candles (in glass) around the garden, and we have some coal-oil lanterns (left over from the war) as well. We had had a couple of spotlights installed on the roof last year to make a bit more light for parties, but now the row of trees along the patio has grown a great deal and somewhat blocks their light.

I taught the whole morning and then went to two teas in the

afternoon; so I must admit that I'm terribly pleased to be sitting this reception out. Zafar is plying me with scotches and bringing up wonderful plates of shrimp, beef kabobs, cheese wrapped in pastry, etc.

Monday, September 23, 1991

THE COCKING DEPARTURE is still being 'celebrated.' We may not survive. Allan is leaving on Thursday, but I will go to the dinner at the British embassy. On Friday Prince Abdullah is having a 'do' at his farm (where we nearly froze last Christmas). But Cockings, Mohammed Al Ariffi, and Allan Lever are insisting that I go. Oh well.

The same day, the Canadian staff is having a party around the pool. Jennifer Galpin is organizing it. We're all to bring munchies. I'll have no trouble contributing, because I expect lots of leftovers from tonight's reception.

I can see on TV that President Bush is speaking live at the United Nations. But the sound isn't working! It was exciting to see Saudi Ambassador Samir al Shihabi elected president of the General Assembly. It gives the Saudis a certain eminence in international affairs. And it's fun to see him on TV in Saudi dress. By the way, Gillian and Siobhan will be interested to know that he is the father-in-law of Nadia al Shihabi, who had tea with them, along with Rema Khashoggi.

Allan has been having his usual busy time. It's gratifying to see that Canadian news hits the Saudi papers almost every day. Allan has had a press briefing regarding the Joint Economic Commission in Canada, and pictures of Saudi and Canadian participants were in all the papers. Then he has been in Sana'a meeting ministers and holding a major reception to introduce our new honorary consul-general, Abdulmalik Zabarah.

From there he went to Jeddah, where I linked up with him to meet a group of 28 senior Canadian high-school students who are aboard a tall ship sailing from Denmark to Capetown. Again he hit the press with pictures and stories. The new Finnish ambassador and his wife, who called on us this week, said Allan seems to be the most active ambassador in Riyadh and that Canada seems to be in the forefront of activities here. Good!

The Canadian student-sailors are having a very interesting time. Our grandson Patrick would be enthralled to hear about their trip. They are having experience in sailing; they have classes aboard the ship too. And they are visiting fascinating places along the way. They have been in Italy, Sardinia, Egypt, and through the Mediterranean and the Suez Canal on the way to the Red Sea.

Surprisingly the Saudis gave them visas and agreed to receive boys and girls (17-year-olds) together. Each got a room in the King's guest palace, and the young people thought they had gone to heaven. You can imagine the bunks, heat, and cramped quarters aboard the sailboat. The Saudis took them to Taif, toured Jeddah, arranged for them to meet university students, etc. Sheikh Talal, our honorary consul-general for Saudi Arabia, very kindly had us all for dinner Friday evening, and it was very pleasant indeed. The students were full of questions and were very impressed with the cleanliness of the countryside and the city. They left yesterday to continue on to Djibouti and Kenya in Africa. Meanwhile, these are kids from all across Canada who are getting to know each other. That's perhaps good for Canada too.

Don Matthews, a Canadian businessman, arrived last night. Since he's travelling alone, Allan invited him to stay with us. He has bad knees (will be going into hospital for surgery when he returns to Canada) so is pleased to be able to exercise in the pool.

He and Allan were off this morning to see Prince Salman, governor of Riyadh. A Saudi business agent will join them for lunch. I haven't heard yet if Matthews will be free to accompany us to the Turkish National Day reception this evening and then to the concert here in the Canadian embassy followed by late supper for about 20 people here.

Last night we left him here to cope with his jet lag while we went for dinner to the home of a very interesting Saudi businessman (with a very British accent — he had spent about 14 years studying in England) and his darling Brazilian wife. (Unfortunately they won't be here at Christmas. I ask every nice person that question so I can be sure the family meet the fun ones. By the way, we had the new Irish ambassador and his wife for lunch. They have two little children here with them — one nine years old and the other three. They will be here.)

Allan is having a dinner party for Mr Matthews tomorrow, and I'm going to Peter and Giselle Liliuses' for a farewell dinner for Wayne House, who is leaving our embassy for a post in Iran.

Meanwhile, I'm so glad to be teaching. It's fun planning the lessons, and it's fun working in such pleasant surroundings and with such engaging students. They had a mid-term exam last week and all passed, so things are going well.

John sounds excited about their new house. David said he had gone to see it last weekend and was so pleased that everyone is enjoying the anticipation of moving into it. David and John visited Nana and Grandpa and found them well. Dad was awfully glad to hear it, because Nana had such a bad cold when he was there.

Institute *of* Public Administration

THE INSTITUTE OF PUBLIC ADMINISTRATION had called me in late September to offer me part-time teaching — an English course for potential secretaries and administrative assistants in banks and hospitals. I would really prefer to teach adults, I thought. And I hadn't yet signed a contract with the French school; I promised to make up my mind by Wednesday. I agreed to examine the institute's course of study. Nice to have options.

In late October 1991 I wrote home to the family. "Next week is going to be busy with a Quebec delegation led by Minister Ciaccia. There will be a reception here in the garden (the weather is perfect for it) and a dinner the following evening. Then Allan goes on to Sana'a with the group."

I went on, "Meanwhile, I'm so glad to be teaching. I'm armed with a certificate for teaching adults and am teaching three mornings a week at the Institute of Public Administration here in Riyadh. The students are all young women — about 20 to 22 years old — and they are really keen. They have sixteen weeks of English before embarking on their administrative courses."

At least three of my students were named Noor, which means 'light.' They assured me that my name, Nora, was in fact the same.

Education for young Saudi women has been limited, even though there are women physicians, professors, and teachers. Many of the privileged few studied in Britain, the United States, or Canada (if a father or brother was able to accompany them abroad).

Now, the Institute — a public institution of higher education — is training women to take positions in women's banks, hospitals, and businesses. These young people were graduates of high school or university, usually married and living with the extended families that looked after their children while they prepared themselves for a new career.

Not all the families were entirely supportive, however. I had long conversations with a woman who sat near the front of the class. She told me her husband was not at all happy to have her at the school. However, she was working hard and hoped that she would be able to accomplish much.

I teach very early in the morning on Saturdays, Sundays, and Tuesdays. That means that I miss the early swim on those days, but I make up for it on the other four days of the week. I'm hoping to be able to show Jill, Siobhan, and Brenda around the school when they are here. The young women are very nice and would certainly get a kick out of meeting my 'daughters'.

Diane Rietz, a special assistant to Minister of International Trade Michael Wilson, arrived a couple of nights ago. She's here in connection with Canadian businessmen's participation in a fair and familiarizing herself with the embassy. Allan got to know her very well last summer, when she was involved in the Saudi exhibition in Montreal and Toronto, so he invited her to stay here.

Siobhan, Jill, and Brenda ready to visit the school

Nora, Jill and Siobhan at the residence

Tuesday, November 5, 1991

ALLAN IS IN YEMEN AGAIN — this time accompanying Quebec Minister of International Affairs (interesting title for a provincial minister!) John Ciaccia and a delegation of officials and businessmen. They were in Riyadh for a few days, so we had a reception for them one evening and a dinner party of 32 people the next. Both events took place in the garden. The weather is perfect these days, and it is beautiful to dine outside.

On Tuesday I'll have a luncheon for 20 or 25 women. I took a thermometer outside while I had my lunch there today. It registered 30 degrees Celsius, which sounds awfully hot to a Canadian, but it was very comfortable in the shade, because the air is so very dry. I think, therefore, that we'll have the luncheon outside too. I'll keep you posted regarding this momentous decision!

The Cockings are arriving to stay with us for four days. You may recall my telling you that we went to what seemed like dozens of farewell parties for them in September. Well, they've been on a round-the-world trip since then and are stopping here on

Residence garden, where dry air makes for cool shade

their way back to England via Damascus. So we'll have to arrange to party some more! At the same time, Alex McGoldrick, the former ambassador of Australia, is arriving to stay with us for four days too. Apparently he's doing business. (I guess they don't have a 'drying-out' period for retired government officials as we do.)

Allan just called from Sana'a. He's had a busy round of meetings today and is preparing to go to a dinner he is hosting. Tomorrow they meet the prime minister of Yemen, attend a luncheon, and pretty well wrap up the trip.

Tonight I'm off to dinner at the palace of Foreign Minister Prince Saud. The hostess is Princess Johara, his wife. It will be a long, drawn-out affair, but I think I'm getting used to them. Anyway, I'm not dreading this as much as I used to. Grania Munro offered to drive (not literally, of course!), so she is coming by at ten to eight.

Tuesday, December 10, 1991

THE FINAL EXAM for the secretarial group I have been teaching is tomorrow. Then there will be a 16-day break. I have enjoyed teaching very much (to my surprise) and expect to more than double my teaching hours next term. I will then be teaching English grammar to two new groups of young women studying hospital administration and also teaching 'listening' in the language lab to another group. Good fun.

The administration asked me what hours I prefer, so I proposed 9:30 a.m.—1:30 p.m., or something like that. That way I could swim every morning before leaving for school. I'll learn my new schedule when I return from Vienna in January. I did lots of preparation in advance so as to free up my holidays.

Nora, Allan, and Sarah at the residence, Christmas 1991

CHAPTER 19

CHRISTMAS *and* NEW YEAR
(1991/92)

Wednesday, December 11, 1991

WHEN I TALKED TO DAVID, he sounded as if he would like a nice, restful holiday. I assured him that we have just the resort for that.

"You can swim, play tennis, lie around and read, go for walks, drive out to the desert — anything you want. We'll arrange for the tennis coach to come a couple of times (in the afternoon) and you can get him to come more often if the mood strikes you. By the way, as you may know, we have two tennis racquets here. Just be sure that two more come with you, so that there can be doubles games whenever anyone feels like it."

I visited a toy store. There is no better way to get in the Christmas mood than checking out all the marvellous toys available. My favourite is still in the Lego / Duplo area. But our gang seemed to have lots of that stuff. I looked for a puzzle for Sarah, but the easy ones seemed too simple. I bought a grown-up puzzle, which can just sit on a card table for anyone to work at any time. By the way, Allan suggested that they ask for playing cards on Saudia during their flight.

"You get to keep them, and we'd be all set for euchre."

Hanif has just made a *huge* sponge-apple cake to serve at a staff meeting this afternoon. All the locally engaged staff are to receive certificates for working through the war.

Speaking of surviving a war and other things, External Affairs has decided to *lower* (!!!) the hardship rating of this post. I suppose that's a way for them to save money. Actually, everyone agrees that the mutawe'en are much more repressive these days than previously. Whoever reads Dad's political reports is not talking to the admin side of the operation. Oh well, the weather makes up for it all.

Hanif is making plans for the embassy Christmas dinner, which will be December 15. He has a businessmen's luncheon for 25 or 30 people to prepare for today, but I have promised him not to entertain anyone between tomorrow and the 15th so that he can prepare things for 80 people. We'll have drinks in the residence, then move over to the atrium in the embassy for the buffet dinner.

We must start on decorations. We are planning to put the tree up on Thursday, and I have bought only a couple of red candles so far. I was at a tea yesterday where the whole house was wonderfully decorated with red tablecloths, candles, ribbons, and wreaths. Good stuff. It was highly motivating.

Mouna Al Rashid had one of her famous music concerts performed by the Suzuki method class of violin students in Riyadh. Her daughter Moudhy played. Decorations were *fabulous*, and she had gone to a lot of trouble to make it very special. She must have flown in a planeload of poinsettias. She knows both Gillian and David and has been in touch with them when she passes through Toronto, but I'm afraid she won't be here over Christmas. Apparently she expects to leave for a skiing holiday in Europe with her children.

We had a week or so of chilly weather, and I thought winter was here till the end of February. But it has warmed up again and is absolutely wonderful!

Friday, December 13, 1991

EARLIER, I HAD A CHAT WITH CHRIS. "Tell everyone that it would be a good idea to pack a bag filled with warm ski jackets etc. so everyone can enjoy an adventure on the desert." Allan had booked the four-wheel recreation vehicle for the Christmas week. I supposed they would have to wear warm clothing as far as New York anyway.

I picked up some books at the British Council library yesterday, and have just finished Doris Lessing's *The Summer before the Dark.* I had heard of the author before, but had never read her books. This was excellent. I can't wait to send Atta for another of hers.

There is a fine exhibition about the Islamic military heritage in the Diplomatic Quarter, which will still be on when the family is here. Allan says he thinks the kids all will enjoy it.

I wrote lots of letters to the family.

Allan is going to Jeddah for a couple of days this week, so we won't have the non-stop dinners to go to — just one on Saturday given by the Russian ambassador and his wife, and one on Tuesday at the home of Paul and Cathy Moreau (a Canadian couple who, unfortunately, won't be here over the Christmas holidays).

My teaching schedule has changed to early Saturday and Sunday mornings, and earlier on Tuesday morning. This may be good because I will be ready to start a long weekend at noon on Tuesday. I am hoping to plan a trip to Cairo in January. We are going to a meeting in Dubai in February, and big holiday in March. The fact that I won't be teaching on Wednesday means that I will be free on Christmas day too. Fancy that!

"HOW WILL THIS WORK?" I had wondered. Saudi Arabia prohibits the practice of any religion other than Islam. Even though some of the embassies had invited their citizens to private religious observances, we had complied with the government edict. But we certainly wanted to have our family visit us over the Christmas holiday season.

Everyone settled in for a stay of one or two weeks. They kept busy swimming, playing tennis, and visiting the gold and carpet markets. In fact, John and Jill both bought lovely rugs — lasting mementos of their time in Saudi Arabia. David and Siobhan were looking keenly at an Iranian rug, but decided to wait a while before making the big purchase.

They found the souks endlessly beguiling. We women covered ourselves

Carpet and jewellery sellers, Riyadh

with abayas and long black headscarves, sallying forth to explore the exquisite Arabian jewellery, featuring 18-carat gold earrings and bracelets, ancient pots, and furnishings. Years later, Abby remembers that she didn't have to wear an abaya because she was only nine years old at the time.

Patrick, Sarah, and Abby couldn't have been better visitors. Patrick recalls that Hanif pulled him aside in the kitchen and said, "Whenever you want a cookie, just climb up onto the counter at this cupboard and help yourself."

Patrick couldn't believe his ears. He questioned, "Even if it is Christmas Eve in the middle of the night?" Solemnly, Hanif nodded his head.

One evening we all went for dinner to the residence of the Pakistani ambassador and his wife, and the kids were just perfect for the whole evening (much to their parents' relief). Another evening we had a dinner party here, and again they were fine. In fact, on New Year's Eve, when we had a potluck buffet for about 60 people, the children took part and fitted in beautifully.

I must describe the New Year's party. It was an annual affair, with different embassies taking turns. This time it was our turn, with mostly diplomats, but also some Saudis, such as Abdullah Dabbagh and Hassan al Jabri and his wife, Salwa. The guiding spirit of it all, who shall be nameless, was *efficient*. She gave instructions about food contributions, designed the Christmas decorations, and gave orders to everyone within shouting distance. The Lever grandchildren were probably appalled, but were clever enough to keep out of her way whenever possible. As grown-ups now they probably still chuckle about that day.

Other days we spent in the desert. With Alan Munro (British ambassador) and Grania, along with their family, we enjoyed picnics British style, with tablecloths and hampers of fine food.

One day a Saudi friend invited us all for lunch in the desert, where tents protected tables heavy with a lavish display of food. Such a good host provided dune buggies too. Chris thought that was the highlight of his trip.

During a sand storm, we visited a camel souk and took pic-

The Levers and Munros prepare a picnic in the desert.

tures that are still a novelty for the Lever family.

Taking my daughters to visit the Institute was memorable for all of us. Sporting our black apparel, we stepped into Atta's waiting car. He drove us smoothly and carefully, very conscious of his precious charges, taking us to the school's front entrance. We entered, set aside our black coverings, and went to the classroom. The young women seemed very happy to meet my accomplished guests — Siobhan, a dermatologist; Brenda, a banker; and Gillian, a treasury analyst with a packaging company. We sat on high stools at the front of the class and responded to a multitude of questions. What a grand opportunity for me to present Canadian women who were working successfully and could be role models for these young Saudi women.

Christmas in the desert with the Munros

Left page: Allan with John and Brenda at Al Diriya. John and Sarah in the desert. Abby and Patrick with Chris at the camel souk. Right page: Gillian in the desert. Abby and Patrick playing in the rocks. Allan in the desert. David at the camel souk with his friends.

Allan and Hugh Mullington in the desert

EPILOGUE
More Adventures

Reprieve!

WE HAD SERVED CANADA as best we could, expecting that our two-year assignment would come to an end in the summer of 1991. Our next move would take us further east possibly to Taiwan. In fact, we travelled to Ottawa for briefings on just such a posting.

Anticipating our imminent departure, Hugh Mullington wrote a gracious note to thank us for the "unstinting support and consideration ... given me during my trips to the Kingdom. It has been a real treat to visit you in Riyadh because I regard you first of all as genuine friends and, secondly, as examples of the finest representatives of our country abroad." We really appreciated his remarks.

He hoped that our next posting would be interesting and cosmopolitan: "No one has deserved it more!"

As it turned out, Prime Minister Brtian Mulroney asked Allan to remain in Saudi Arabia, saying how much he appreciated his experience and his invaluable participation in Canadian businessmen's negotiations for contracts with the Saudi government. We would be staying in Riyadh!!!

And so we welcomed the continuing opportunity to enjoy diplomacy and friendships in this fascinating Kingdom for two more years. We finally left Riyadh in the summer of 1993.

'Second City' *and* Home

As it turned out, our next posting was, in Hugh's words, both interesting and cosmopolitan. Allan became Canadian consul-general in Chicago. We spent four years in that amazing 'second city,' where Allan promoted Canadian trade and we both enjoyed the Chicago Symphony, the Art Institute, and the Lyric Opera. Our years in Chicago were inspiring. After Allan retired from the Canadian diplomatic service, he became president of Chicago's World Trade Center.

During the last few years Allan has still been busy. Now in Toronto, he serves on corporate and church boards, travels to Saudi Arabia from time to time, and heads up a ministry for growth and innovation in St Andrew's Presbyterian Church downtown.

Meanwhile, I have enjoyed my association with the Toronto Symphony Volunteer Committee and its various projects and fund-raisers in support of our wonderful Toronto Symphony Orchestra. As its past co-president and secretary for many terms, I have worked with other volunteers on speakers' series, bridge events, art auctions, piano competitions, and fine-wine auctions.

And last Christmas Allan and I spent a couple of fun-filled days in a 'stay-cation' in Toronto with 22 of us — children, spouses, grandchildren and friends, great-grandchildren (!) — all gathering for a hockey game, visits to an aquarium and an art gallery, and lots of food, glorious food!

Chicago waterfront

Tumari Gate, Riyadh

POSTSCRIPT

Twenty-five Years Later

PEOPLE OFTEN EXPRESS INTEREST about our time in Saudi Arabia. "Are women still not driving?" they often ask.

"Not yet, although there really has been progress over the time since I was there. There are rumours even now that women may find themselves behind the steering wheel in the next six months."

But women are increasingly taking part in the political and economic life of the Kingdom. The Institute of Public Administration, where I taught those bright, enthusiastic young women, now graduates many females to fill posts in banks, hospitals, universities, and commercial enterprises. Women sit on corporate boards and city councils, serve as members of chambers of commerce, and are guaranteed one-fifth of the places on the Kingdom's appointed Majlis Ash-Shura (Shura Council, or Consultative Assembly).

The oil-rich country had been dependent on foreign workers to service its slowly growing economy. Even while we were living in Riyadh, the Kingdom was developing a "Saudiization" program to encourage its own people to enter the job market (think of the Institute of Public Administration), while Prince Abdullah headed the Royal Commission for Jubail and Yanbu, which spurred diversification.

Allan has returned to the Kingdom several times. As he enters hotels now, Saudi women as well as men on the hotel staff greet him. This is a change from the 1990s when I was there.

The population of Saudi Arabia has grown by leaps and bounds. Riyadh alone now has eight million people — quadruple the two million during our stay.

Imagine the changes in communication. When the buildup to the Gulf War began, the Saudis had just state-run television and radio, filled mostly with religious programming. The government let in CNN, as I mentioned above, only in 1991.

I recall a conversation with Nick Cocking at a dinner table one evening all those years ago. He told us, "The American military have been developing something called the internet. With general use of this new technology, people all over the world will eventually be able to communicate with each other." Well, yes! And Nick has recently contacted me on Facebook to be his "Friend"! Riyadh's people now enjoy all the benefits of social media, as well as TV stations worldwide.

During his travels to Riyadh, Allan enjoys seeing long-time associates such as Sheik Teymour Alireza, Dr Ahmed al Malik, and Sheik Mohammed Al Fraih. He has also worked closely with Basem al Shihabi, the architect of the Tuwaiq Palace.

On many visits, Allan has had the opportunity to continue his association with Prince Sultan bin Salman, the first Arab astronaut and now the very active president and chair of the Board of the Saudi Commission for Tourism and National Heritage (two-pronged diversification!). In November 2012, Prince Sultan hosted the of-

Prince Sultan bin Salman

ficial opening of his organization's spectacular exhibition "The Roads of Arabia: Archaeology and History of the Kingdom of Saudi Arabia" at the Smithsonian Institution in Washington, DC. Allan received an invitation, and the prince greeted him warmly and presented him with a deluxe edition of the very handsome catalogue.

Prince Sultan's father, Prince Salman (bin Abdulaziz al Saud), then governor of Riyadh, had led the delegation presenting "The Kingdom Yesterday and Today" that travelled to Canada in 1991 at Allan's urging. Prince Salman is now King of Saudi Arabia — Custodian of the Two Holy Mosques!

One of our Saudi friends, Prince Abdullah, whom we visited at his farm in the desert, recently served as Saudi ambassador in Washington — perhaps his nation's top diplomatic post.

Meanwhile, I have been corresponding with the Hutchingses and the Galpins. After Saudi Arabia, David Hutchings was posted to Germany and then to Somalia, before he and Mary retired to Halifax and, more recently, Montreal. They keep in close touch with Don and Judy McLennan and Ron and Bernadette Bollman, passing along good wishes between us.

Jennifer and Albert Galpin returned to Ottawa, where Albert spent several years at External Affairs welcoming visiting delegations to our country. Kristianne, the dear little girl born during the Scud attack, was later joined by siblings, to make a full family circle.

These wonderful friends' letters have meant a great deal to me, bringing back precious memories of the years we spent in Saudi Arabia — the tensions of the months leading to and culminating in the Gulf War and, more important, the opportunities to learn so much from ambassadors' wives, dear Saudi friends, and even strangers, who welcomed us with open arms. What an opportunity for both diplomacy and friendship!

ACKNOWLEDGMENTS

O VER THE YEARS, I must admit, I showed my notes for this book to no one. Our four children and their spouses, however — John and Brenda, David and Siobhan, Gillian and Kevin, and Christopher and Kathy — would be familiar with some of these pages: I based them partly on the letters I sent them and on our faxes and long-distance telephone conversations. And, of course, they visited us several times in Riyadh. They and their (then) youngsters were incredibly supportive of us during our long time away from home. We will be forever grateful for their vital participation, and their empathy and kindness to us, all these years.

I played with my prose from time to time, and one summer, while visiting my sister Ruth Hutchinson at her cottage in the Kawartha Lakes, I made the trip daily to Fleming College's Haliburton School of the Arts, in the town of Haliburton, for Nora Zylstra Savage's course in writing memoirs.

Nora suggested that conversation adds interest to a story.

"Well, let me try," said I. "We'll see how it works."

Allan very patiently agreed to have a look at what I had written. He was terrific in pointing out particular details and remembering with relish further stories of our escapades in the Kingdom.

And when Words Indeed publisher/editor John Parry and designer/composer/typesetter Anne Vellone of Vellone Design agreed to review my manuscript and expressed such enthusiasm, I was astonished and very moved. It has been a pleasure to work with them both. They have been hard taskmasters; but I have appreciated their ministrations while they have so generously given of their own time, talents, and extremely diligent work to put this project together. I am deeply grateful to them.

Anne Vellone coaxed many photographs out of us that Allan and I did not realize we had. Now that I see them complementing my prose, I can hardly believe how precious they are. Anne also spent many scores of hours researching, sourcing, and editing images to depict our magical years in the Kingdom and the amazing natural and architectural highlights of the Arabian peninsula.

Renowned political journalist and writer Stevie Cameron has kindly written a generous foreword. We came to know Stevie in Ottawa when we were there. In Toronto, she has been a pillar of St Andrew's Presbyterian's Out of the Cold Program; she also shared her skills and empathy on Vancouver's East Side during her eight years researching and writing there.

John Holtby kindly allowed us to quote (pp. xxi—xxii) from his *Globe and Mail* account of my crucial House of Commons roll call in November 1984, and we quote from my abaya article (pp. 15—16) in External Affairs magazine *Liaison* (April 1990), 16—17, with permission of Global Affairs Canada, Service, Ottawa, 20147. Aonghus Kealy put the 'joy' in the press release.

Thanks re Al-Qaysumah to Dr Laura Brandon, to Professor Roger Sarty, and to Susan Ross at the Canadian War Museum (CWM). It is an honour to include CWM images from the Canadian field hospital at Al-Qaysumah (pp. 187—8) by a living, official Canadian war artist (for the Gulf War), Edward (Ted) Zuber. Zuber is the only Canadian with service medals from Korea and the Gulf War.

PUBLISHER'S NOTE

A Desert Whirlwind

John Parry

A T CHRISTMAS 2016, Nora Lever's neighbour Tony van Strauben-zee gave her and Allan a copy of his *Rind in the Marmalade: A Headhunter's Tales*, from Words Indeed. Reading that apparently inspired Nora to turn her Riyadh diaries into a book. She approached me in January 2017 with a manuscript, which I devoured and decided instantly to ask her permission to publish.

Designer Anne Vellone and I had a delightful meeting with Nora and Allan in their beautiful apartment and learned about their years in Riyadh and since. Their exquisite mementos from the Arabian peninsula and their beautiful library overwhelmed us, and we showed them our previous book, *Recollections of a Neighbourhood: Huron-Sussex from UTS to Stop Spadina*, which had been 26 years in the making, though only 3½ for me and 2 for Anne.

Turning Nora's manuscript into a book would take less than six months — but what a whirlwind! Anne and I were dealing with experts: a possible cover design featured — as Allan pointed out instantly — an Omani jar, not right for a memoir of Saudi Arabia!

Anne's insistent questioning brought out many lovely photos from Nora and Allan that they had forgotten about. Nora was also very open to Anne's instinct to enhance her powerful stories with rich visual images — particularly architectural — from that stark and striking world. Nora and Allan's granddaughter Maggie Lever, MFA, took the stunning author's photo for the cover.

As for production itself, Anne and I would like to thank Steve McClinton, district sales manager, Canada, for Mohawk; and Chris Whitern, business development representative for Ariva. Special gratitude to Dimas and his crew at Andora Graphics, who, with patience, dedication, and skill, printed the book you are reading.

On the editorial front, I was thrilled to see Nora's very thoughtful 1990 article on wearing the abaya for an External Affairs magazine for diplomats. These talented people and their families may go to parts of the world where a sensitive, intelligent observer wants to ask many pointed questions, and that format encouraged them to do so and invited thoughtful responses. Stevie Cameron, in her touching foreword, and our several deeply knowledgeable reviewers, raised more questions.

I kept bugging Nora about the Canadian medical facility she and Allan visited during the Gulf War. Where was it? I found out about the Canadian field hospital at Al-Qaysumah, and Allan eventually confirmed that that was it. Anne was able, late in production, to fit in two images from Al-Qaysumah by Ted Zuber, Canada's only official war artist from the Gulf War.

I'm not sure how Nora and Allan feel about our whirlwind process, but for Anne and me it's been a fascinating journey of discovery.

LIST *of* ILLUSTRATIONS

Masmak Fort, historic centre, Riyadh

© javarman / Bigstock. Page 57.
© HomoCosmicos / Bigstock. Page 57.
© Datsenko Maryna / Shutterstock. Page 61.
© Akika / Bigstock. Page 63.
© Elisabeth2010 / iStock by Getty Images. Page 64.
© abalcazar / iStock by Getty Images. Page 69.
© Trinity Mirror / Mirrorpix / Alamy Stock Photo. Page 71.
© imageBROKER / Alamy Stock Photo. Page 91.
© Oleg Znamenskiy / Bigstock. Page 91.
© Fedor Selivanov / Shutterstock. Page 93.
© JM Travel Photography / Bigstock. Page 95.
© RnDmS / Bigstock. Page 96.
© swisshippo / Bigstock. Page 102.
© tenzinsherab / iStock by Getty Images. Page 103.
© B. O'kane / Alamy Stock Photo. Page 103.
© B. O'kane / Alamy Stock Photo. Page 103.
© Reuters / Alamy Stock Photo. Page 106.
© MediaPunch Inc / Alamy Stock Photo. Page 127.
© Julian Nieman / Alamy Stock Photo. Page 137.
© drpyan / Shutterstock. Page 153.
© Z2A1 / Alamy Stock Photo. Page 159.
© ITAR-TASS Photo Agency / Alamy Stock Photo. Page 162
© karenfoleyphotography / iStock by Getty Images. Page 180.
© kevinebrine / Bigstock. Page 183.
Al Qaysumah, by Ted Zuber (acrylic on canvas), 19960062-007,
    page 187, and *Col. Claude Auger* — First Canadian Field Hospital,
    by Ted Zuber (graphite on paper), 19960062-038, page 188;
    both works in Beaverbrook Collection of War Art, Canadian
    War Museum (CWM), Ottawa.
© Johnny Saunderson / Alamy Stock Photo. Page 193.
© Julian Nieman / Alamy Stock Photo. Page 197.
© Joseph Sohm / Shutterstock. Page 203.
© Johnny Saunderson / Alamy Stock Photo. Page 205
© Laborant / Shutterstock. Page 208.
© B.O'Kane / Alamy Stock Photo. Page 234
© Julian Nieman / Alamy Stock Photo. Page 235.
© Eunika Sopotnicka / Shutterstock. Page 243.
© Art Directors & TRIP / Alamy Stock Photo. Page 244.
© swisshippo / Bigstock. Page 254.
© Gimas / Bigstock. Page 256.
© Ovchinnikova Irina / Shutterstock. Page 257.
© Gimas / Bigstock. Page 262.

Murraba Palace, Riyadh

A symbol of Yemen: Dar al-Hajar (Rock Palace) (1930s), summer residence, built by ruler Imam Yahya atop 18th-century ruins. Wadi Zahr, near Sana'a

CANADA DAY!

"Canada 125 Years / Le Canada 125 ans"!
In 1992, to mark this special anniversary
of Confederation, Nora and Allan invited
a lively crew to celebrate with them in the
Canadian embassy in Riyadh. Hanif, members of the household and diplomatic staff,
expatriates, and their excited children
watch the ambassador and his wife cut the
huge, bilingual cake sporting the Maple
Leaf flag. Twenty-five years later, the couple were still in touch with a number of
these families and were thrilled to launch
this memoir of their years in the Kingdom
on Canada's 150th birthday, 1 July 2017.

Celebrating Canada Day, 1992

EDITION N⁰ 1

DESIGNER ANNE VELLONE
composed, designed & depicted
DIPLOMACY AND FRIENDSHIP in
Toronto, Canada. ANDORA GRAPHICS
printed & bound 1000 copies on MOHAWK
paper, using ARNHEM typeface designed
by a first generation, Dutch digital type
designer, FRED SMEIJERS, *circa 1999*
— a very legible serif with an edge.
VELLONE DESIGN *c.* 2017

vellone**design**

Inside Masmak Fort, historic centre,
Riyadh, Saudi Arabia